Do You Believe?

A Meditation on Faith

WILLIAM E. MARSH

authorHOUSE®

AuthorHouse™
1663 Liberty Drive
Bloomington, IN 47403
www.authorhouse.com
Phone: 833-262-8899

Published by AuthorHouse 10/08/2020

ISBN: 978-1-6655-0047-0 (sc)
ISBN: 978-1-6655-0046-3 (e)

Introduction

As many a person has observed, we humans have a burning need, a relentless compulsion, to believe. To believe in *something*. We cannot live without believing. But how are we to understand this? While it is easy enough to believe that, for instance, the sky is blue when the sun is shining, or that women give birth to babies, it is far more difficult to believe something that we cannot see.

But we do this all the time, don't we? Every ...moment of every day we believe in things that we cannot see. Almost all of us believe that there is a Mt. Everest in the Himalayas in Nepal. Most of us believe that there are various subatomic particles inside an atom. And almost everyone believes that there is a city in Russia named Moscow. Yet most of us have never "seen" these things.

Yet we believe that they are there. People who have stood on the summit of Mt. Everest have shared their photographs. People who participate in the experiments conducted in the Tevatron at Fermilab outside of Chicago or the Large Hadron Collider housed underneath the border of France and Switzerland have shown us visual evidences of the quarks, muons, gluons, and other particles that bounce around inside an atom. And anyone who has been to Moscow can tell anyone who has not that, yes, Moscow is definitely there.

What about, however, things that, try as we might, we simply cannot see in or from this world? I think here about things like angels and goblins, Nirvana and Heaven, Mother Mary and God, and all other phenomena supernatural. Unless we stumble into a wormhole or slice of interstitial space, we are not likely to see them. If we believe in any of these things, we therefore do so without having visible evidence that they are there.

That's a problem, isn't it? And it's not just a problem for the believer. It's a problem for the unbeliever, too. While a believer must find reasons and evidences to justify her belief in things she cannot see in this world see, an unbeliever must conversely wonder why otherwise perfectly rational people choose to believe in a world of the unseen. Either way, belief in the invisible and intangible creates problems. It always has. And it always will. Indeed, it cannot help *but* doing so: belief tends to divide as much as it unites.

Think about belief as faith. As we have noted, we all believe in things whether we have immediate visual evidence for them or not. And most of us go one step further and *trust* them, too. We may trust them for our happiness, understanding, health, livelihood, even our life. We do so because even if *we* have not seen such things, someone has. We have evidence. Or so we think.

When we trust, we exercise faith. Oh no, some may respond: faith is believing in the absence of evidence. Yes, that is one definition. If we journey into faith's linguistic past, however, if we travel back through the many discussions of the word "faith" in the centuries before us, we see that, in its original sense, faith means to trust. Which we all do: every moment of every day. Like it or not, we all are, in some form or fashion, creatures of faith.

But there's faith and there's faith. The book before you does not explore the black and white faith we use every day, the facile assumptions we make to deal with life's various quibbles and challenges. It rather examines the faith we use to believe, and trust, in things that are, gasp, supernatural. Things that no one has seen; things that are invisible to us. Things to which most of us turn when life's issues become too perplexing, too complicated, too much to bear with the tools of a material world. This faith takes us beyond ourselves. Indeed, it takes us beyond this world. It pushes us into realms and conditions of experience we finite creatures cannot fully understand. Conditions for which we have no visible evidence. It's not easy.

Nor should it be: it trusts the truth of the unseen. Is it rational? It is. Is it logical? Not always. Is it true? Always. This faith is therefore a decision. It is a decision to trust. It's a decision to trust in a God who loves, a God who cares, a God who is present and actively and purposefully working in every part of the cosmos.

A God, however, whom we cannot see.

Yet it is this God in whom I have believed for over forty-six years. Do I occasionally wonder why I do? Sure. Do I frequently wrestle with my belief? Of course. Again: faith isn't easy. But that's why I wrote this book. Yes, it's difficult to trust in an unseen presence. Absolutely. It's also very wonderful, perhaps the most wonderful of all experiences in this life. Why? This book is my effort, at this point in my life, to answer this question. It is a meditation on my attempts, attempts that I make over and over again in the course of this book's narrative, to come to grips, emotionally, spiritually, and intellectually, with what I repeatedly call the "dark light" of faith. It's a story of seeing and not seeing, believing and not believing. It's a story in which truth's fullness always eludes me.

But it's also a story of conviction. A conviction that, all things considered, God is there. And that he is a God absolutely and unreservedly worth trusting. Regardless of the cost.

Join me.

Do You Believe?
A Meditation on Faith

Over forty years ago, on a cloudless Thursday afternoon, I was hiking with an old friend in the hills above Thousand Oaks, California. I had not seen her in over three years. We had met in the early Seventies, when I was living in the mountains surrounding Jasper, Alberta, in the northern Canadian Rockies. Now I was living in Southern California, attending seminary, trying to master and come to grips with the theological nuances of the Christian faith into which I had recently come.

Very much spiritually minded, but not terribly religious, a product of a family of eight in a small town about a hundred miles east of Jasper, Sherrill was probing the boundaries of what I thought I had come to believe. I had no trouble believing that she would identify with the sentiments embodied in British poet William Blake's oft cited "Auguries of Innocence," namely, "To see a World in a Grain of Sand, and a Heaven in a Wild Flower, hold Infinity in the palm of your hand, and Eternity in an hour."

The world is its own vision.

I found most of what Sherrill asked me fairly easy to

answer. Questions about the person and work of Jesus, my view of the church I was then attending, what God says about moral failure and transgression, well, the answers came quickly. After all, I was into my second year of studying them. It was almost, I say with a touch of irreverence, child's play.

But then she dug deeper. Much deeper. "What about predestination? Why does God choose some and not others?"

Ouch. Of all the doctrines I had been studying, predestination was easily the most confounding. Why indeed does God choose only some people to be saved? Why will only the "elect" enjoy heavenly bliss with their creator? What does this say about God? About his love?

After looking at Sherrill blankly for a few seconds and pondering, with no small amount of trepidation, how to respond, I finally said, "I can't answer that. I simply do not know what to say."

I was being thoroughly honest. Painfully honest. Yes, I believe that I can find the notion of predestination (broadly defined) presented in the Bible. But when I try to decide what it suggests about humans and God and God's love for his human creation, I can find no clear answers. Other than to say that God knows what he is doing. Or that, as John Calvin might say, it is a mystery into which we should not tread. Or to say, with Deuteronomy 29:29 that, "The secret things belong to the Lord our God, but the things revealed belong to us and to our sons forever, that we may observe all the words of this law." God has revealed to us what we need to know, and that's *all* we need to know. We have the Law, God's word, the eternally loving God's instructions and directives for living rightly, before us. That's enough.

Easy, for many a believer, to say. But the believer has, as Cinderella (in truth, her given name is Cyndee), a dear college friend with whom I correspond, in fifteen and twenty page single spaced pages, about once a year, often points out to me, "eyes to see." Absolutely. Numerous studies affirm that people who believe will, through years and decades of worship, study, and prayer, in fact, usually in an unconscious way, "train" or "rework" their brains to "see" theological conversation in a manner that tends to confirm what they already believe. We should not be surprised at this conclusion. In many ways, it's simply a restatement of how our "confirmation bias" tends to shape, again, in ways we may not always realize, how we respond to a given life situation. Deeply held beliefs do that.

To a person "outside" the faith, however, saying that, in essence, "Only God knows, and this is as it should be," is hardly satisfactory. How can it be? It is a statement of an already convicted faith. The British philosopher Bertrand Russell, a person who all his life committed to determining what he can know without any rational doubt (and who, even though he was a mathematician, was uncomfortable with how we must admit that mathematical axioms are inherently true) once said,

> "The point I am concerned with is that, if you are quite sure there is a difference between right and wrong, then you are then in this situation: is that difference due to God's fiat or is it not? If it is due to God's fiat, then for God himself there is no difference between right and wrong, and it

is no longer a significant statement to say
that God is good."

What is Lord Russell's point? He is suggesting that if
we make God the final and absolute standard of good, what
we are in fact saying is that we really have no way to know
what is good other than to say that, well, God is good. And
we have no way to prove that God is good other than to say
that he is good. It is quite circular.

Moreover, as Russell's statement also implies, how does
God, and only God, know what is good, anyway?

That's why, apart from believing that, on the basis of the
biblical testimony and our personal experience, God is good,
we really cannot prove that he is. Hence, if I had told Sherrill
that, well, in terms of predestination, you just need to trust
God because he is good, I'd offering her an essentially dead-
end argument. Unless she believes and accepts that God is
trustworthy, true, and loves her, she will not be satisfied.

After we said goodbye to each other at the end of the
day, I realized, not for the first time, but certainly in a fresh
way, one of the greatest challenges of faith. We will not
believe unless we understand, yet we will sometimes not
understand until we believe. We're always being asked to
trust in what we do not know.

It's the cruelest "Sophie's Choice" of all.

Simple? Hardly. For the past nine years, I have attended
a monthly discussion group and gathering of atheists,
humanists, and agnostics. We meet at a Unitarian church.
I learned of the group when, wanting the students in
my world religions class to hear from adherents of other
religious traditions firsthand, I contacted the pastor of this

church. After we met, my interest in Unitarianism further piqued, my wife, Carol, and I went to services the following Sunday. In reading the church bulletin for that week, I noted that at 7:00 p.m. the upcoming Tuesday, this atheist-humanist-agnostic (AHA) group would meet. Intrigued even more and, as always, ever eager to interact with those whose religious or philosophical views differ from mine, I resolved to go.

Once the people in the group realized I was not there to browbeat them into believing in Christianity but rather to learn in mutual exchange of viewpoint, they accepted (with one exception, a rather ornery individual who was not just an atheist but, as other members put it, an "anti-theist") me. Over the years, I've given several presentations on philosophy, religion, and the like. All have been received positively. Some attendees have even read a couple of my books. All in all, it's been fascinating and enlightening. And I've made some good friends. Even though we understand that our starting points and conclusions about reality are *very* different, we accept each other's freedom to believe what he or she chooses. We do not argue. It would be pointless. The gap (actually, it's more an abyss) is too great. In fact, it's impassable.

A few years ago, however, during a discussion we were having about the role of humanism in deciphering the meaning of religion, I found myself responding to some hard questions. I thought of not just my conversation with Sherrill, but of those I had had with many other people along the way. No one that night was antagonistic; they just wanted, I think, to hear what I had to say.

"Do you believe the Bible is inspired?" Well, yes. "Why?"

The short answer is to say that, as 2 Timothy 3:16 states, "All Scripture is inspired [literally, 'God-breathed'] by God." But that, as I realized my very first day in seminary, proves very little. To say that the Bible is inspired because it says that it is inspired, well, what sort of logic is this?

I tried to check off the usual boxes: the astonishing concordance of events described in the Bible with extant archaeological evidence; the very low amount of variance and change in the biblical text over the many centuries of its composition and dissemination; the Bible being one of the most widely attested historical documents of the ancient world; the way that, throughout history, the Bible has spoken to all kinds of people all over the world in ways that various Avestas, Vedas, observations of the I Ching, teachings of the Buddha, Native American spirituality, and the Qur'an have not; and, perhaps most important, how some verses from the Bible so powerfully moved me to the point where, over forty-six years ago, I was willing to believe in Jesus and God.

My final point, I added, underscores the central issue. The Bible is a human record, yes, but it is a human record guided, shaped, and moved by a supernatural presence. It is a record of divine encounter. In fact, it *is* encounter: encounter with God. The Bible, I concluded, echoes and reflects its cultural, historical, and literary settings, but it does so under the agency and guidance of an eternal God.

In this, I added, the Bible is truth.

Is this a mouthful? You bet it is. Did it convince anyone in my discussion group? Certainly not. Does it convince you? I have no way of knowing.

Needless to say, I am a creation of my color, geography,

upbringing, experiences, and class. I did not enter into my Christian faith in an epistemological vacuum. Had I grown up in another part of the world, one shaped by the teachings of the Buddha, the Vedas, or the Qur'an, I would surely view Christianity very differently. I would surely have responded differently to the words of the Bible that were presented to me that October night in Jasper National Park those many decades ago. For me to therefore claim that, as I sit in my white middle class American vantage point in the political and religious safety of the West, those words I heard that night would have spoken to me regardless of where I had been, well, that may be a stretch. Of course, I could say that had I been coming from a different place culturally, God would have chosen different words—and different people to voice them—to move my heart.

But this avoids the more fundamental issue. It does not answer why I feel I'm justified in saying that my faith experience is the most important one. And it fails to address how, in light of the impossibly difficult to unravel idea of God being good because God is good (or God being trustworthy because God is trustworthy), belief in the Christian God is nonetheless thoroughly logical.

It's a tough nut to crack.

In his Siddhartha, a novel which many a wanderer in the Sixties and Seventies, which I was, "took up and read," to draw a line from Augustine's Confessions, German writer Hermann Hesse presents a fictional journey, based on his understanding of real life events, of how the one we call Buddha became the Buddha. As Hesse, drawing from many centuries of writing, speculation, and belief, tells the story, days before his mother gave birth to Siddhartha, she and his father heard a prophecy that their son would grow up to be either a rich prince or a penurious monk. Well accustomed to a life of affluence and privilege, Siddhartha's parents certainly did not wish for him to go in another direction. Their son, they resolved, would not be a monk. From the moment Siddhartha came into the world, his parents proceeded to shower him with all the opulence that money could buy. They hoped that, steeped in the blessings of wealth, their son would never think to stray from it.

It didn't work out that way. Although Siddhartha grew up being happy, got married, and had a son, he subsequently began to wonder whether this was all there is. He had never left the palace grounds. What lay beyond these high walls? Subsequently, one fine morning, without telling anyone, the young prince woke up, gathered a few belongings, and hit the road.

As he walked, he saw three things. The first was an old man, decrepit and weary. Siddhartha was shocked: do people really get old?

He next saw a sick person, a gaunt and emaciated man wallowing in his own excreta. Another shock: do people, Siddhartha thought, actually get sick?

As he was recovering from these two dissonances, Siddhartha came upon a dead body. A corpse. He had never seen death. In fact, he had never heard it mentioned. The prince was beside himself: will I really get old? Will I really get sick?

And will I really die?

As he is wrestling with these predictions of weakness and mortality, Siddhartha encounters a monk. To the troubled young prince, this monk seems the picture of peace: quiet, humble, in apparently perfect alignment with the universe. Siddhartha immediately concludes that it is the monk whom he wishes to be. The monk, he thinks, has everything together. He needs nothing more. Siddhartha's path is now clear. He must pursue the experience out of which the monk's equanimity comes: enlightenment.

As the story continues, Siddhartha arrives at a river. As the querulous prince sits down and watches this river, watches it flow and flow and flow, he comes to some pivotal insights. Life, he decides, is like a river, an endlessly flowing river. In this river, this river that, to his mind, seems to be illuminating every event and facet of existence with a rich glow of supernal understanding, life presents itself most clearly, manifests itself most deeply. It unfolds itself as it is. Life, Siddhartha therefore decides, is always moving, always expanding, always growing. But it is always standing still, too: it's always here, yet it's never anywhere. Life goes around as much as it comes around. Wealth and poverty; fame and ignominy; age, sickness, and death: none really matter. Life will always be; life will never not be.

And we're just passing through, he observes, a single, unbearably tiny current in a supremely vast stream of existence. We're wisps, tiny, tiny gossamer wisps of space and time. Furthermore, although one day we will end, we in fact will not. We will empty ourselves of all suffering, yes, and leave the material world. We will be nothingness. But it is a highly fecund nothingness. It lives; it lives forever. As will we. We will no longer be "here," but we will no longer be "there," either. We will just "be." As will life.

It was Heraclitus's point all over again.

This insight became Siddhartha's bedrock act of faith.

Nothing would ever again exceed it for him as a picture of wisdom, hope, or reality. On it he lived his life; on it he entered into death. With this, Siddhartha believed that he had set himself free from the world and its sickness, aging, death, and pain. He was freed from time, he was freed from eternity. He would flow and flow forever.

Is this insight mine? No. Can I accept it? Sure. Can I believe it? Sure.

But can I say it is truth?[1] That is the far bigger question. When I backpack, as I've been doing for over fifty years, I love drinking the mountain water. I cannot wait to fill and drink from my water bottle in the morning; I cannot wait to fill and drink from it in the afternoon. In a ways, water is the *Urstoff* of my mountain existence. It grounds my day; it ties it together; it makes it whole.

In a good mountain summer, a summer preceded by an above average winter snowfall, water is literally everywhere. Lakes are filled to bursting, rivers are torrents, meadows feel damp and spongy even on the sunniest of days. Flowers bloom profusely, trees sparkle with verdancy, and rarely is an evening quiet, even at the highest elevations. Whether they move hidden under a snowpack or gurgle in the open air, the rivers keep flowing through the night, sunset to dawn, prattling their way to eternity.

So many afternoons I have spent hanging in my camp, trail miles behind me for the day, sitting by a river or lake,

---

[1] Because this is not intended to be a scholarly treatise, I leave for another day the far more complicated question of what truth fundamentally is. Be it the product of correspondence or coherence, truth, particularly in a world infused with phenomenal as well as noumenal, remains a rather slippery thing.

sipping water, listening to the rhythms of the moment. I look at the mountains, I gaze at the trees, I poke holes in the sky. Everything joins; everything that is anything, earth, water, sky, and sun converge, running together in perfect harmony. All is well, all is well. My life becomes an ocean, an ocean of cosmic, unfathomable wonder, a vast and rumbling sea, continuously boring into the deepest recesses of my imagination.

How could anything be so beautiful?

For this reason, I do not find it too difficult to believe that in watching a river, a river of fresh, clear water flowing on and on and on, Siddhartha found his ultimate spiritual insight, that in the rhythms of running water he found his enlightenment. It's not dissimilar to the assertions of a friend of mine who tells us that she finds her "church" in nature, that when she steps into a forest and begins hiking, she feels singularly happy and free. Nothing else matters.

She doesn't need anything else. My faith says, however, that I do.

It's a vexing conundrum.

A few years ago, Carol and I spent a long weekend in the town of Stinson Beach in California's Marin County. Saturday morning, we visited an art gallery. One piece immediately caught my eye. Sculpted by a rabbi who lived in San Francisco, it was titled "Tree of Life." Set in a piece of Sierra granite, a tree, several strands of wire that had been carefully shaped into a trunk and limbs, rose up, spreading itself over the rock. To me, it was a vision of grace, a picture of lucidity, clarity, and perfect balance: I knew I had to have it.

The next day we returned to the gallery and made the

purchase. Now the Tree is in our home, set on a table at a window into which the morning sun comes each day. Summer or winter, it sparkles brilliantly, never failing to remind us that light is lovely, timely, and ever present. A friend of mine calls it the "sparkle of God."

This friend is a rabbi, a person with whom I have spent many hours discussing the differences—and similarities—between Judaism and Christianity. Like I do, he believes in God, and like I do, he believes that the Bible (at least the Old Testament or, as he puts it, the Tanakh) is truth. Jonathan will love God, the God in whom we both believe, until the day he dies.

And beyond.

To love God, Jonathan says, is to keep his commandments, the precepts of the Torah, the Law. The 613 commandments in the Torah, he says, give him "613 ways to love" God. By keeping the Torah, Jonathan believes he is loving God.

At the heart of this is doing good deeds. Judaism, Jonathan says, is the only major religion of the world that makes doing good deeds its foundational and operative truth. It's an intriguing argument. Islam and Christianity, to name the other two major monotheistic religions of the world, certainly hold doing good deeds paramount to spiritual health and calling. Yet both make other transformational commitments, be they submitting oneself to Allah or trusting one's salvation to Jesus, as essential precursors to it. Not that one can't do good deeds without making these commitments, just that centering them in a life allegiance to Allah or Jesus gives them, from an Islamic or Christian viewpoint, eternal value.

Yet this just takes us back to square one. Whose truth is "truth"? If I say, as most Christians do, that Jesus is the only way to find God, I am also saying that anyone who does not agree with this is wrong, indeed, absolutely wrong. This is hard, very hard. Everyone I know would agree I'm a fairly easy going person. When I take a position like this, a position which some see as frighteningly dogmatic, however, I appear to be anything but that. I become my own worst nightmare, a living embodiment of intolerance, pride, and discord. As Sherrill pointed out to me that afternoon in the hills above Thousand Oaks, it's an affront to her dignity: how can I say that I am always and forevermore right?

Besides, spirituality isn't just for Christians. Humans are inherently spiritual beings.

In a series of novels he wrote in the mid-Seventies, Calvin Miller depicted Jesus as a Singer, a Singer whose Song moves and captures peoples' hearts. When the Singer plays his Song, everyone hears it; few can turn away, even fewer can refuse to accept it. For most people who encounter the Singer and his Song, life is never the same. They are, we are told, made new, never to be their "past" selves again.

While for some this might bring to mind the Pied Piper or Orwellian visions of mind control, and perhaps rightly so, if we think about this scenario as portraying God as music we all cannot help, if only for a moment in our lives, but hear, we put it in a much different light. If God is there, and if we believe that, however we do so, he is, it seems that we would find what he says to us to be so deeply compelling that we would have great difficulty in ignoring it. It's akin to German philosopher Rudolph Otto's idea, which he proposed over a century ago, that we human beings are "fascinated" with things transcendent and divine. So powerfully attractive do we find the divine, or as he puts it, the "mysterium tremendum," that, though we may be afraid of it, we cannot help but be drawn to it. It's a song we cannot turn off.

Consider, however, an observation of Franz Kafka. "The meaning of life," Kafka said, "is that it stops." He has a point. In many ways, it is often easier to imagine life as something that, one day, simply stops. It is simpler to picture existence as something into which we are born, enjoy, then leave forever. For one, we wouldn't need to worry about who is right. Nor would we need to concern ourselves with things we cannot physically see, things like God, heaven, or angels. Moreover, although we would still experience our share of puzzlements or questions, we would not be worried about what God is doing, if anything, in or about them. We could live, and then, one day, stop living, all the while understanding that we will find our meaning, as Kafka suggests, in exactly that. We would live for a today without worrying about a tomorrow. Life would be markedly less complicated. The music plays; the music stops playing: simple as that.

Moreover, as David Starr Jordan, the founder of modern taxonomy, once wrote, "There is grandeur in this view of life." Even if we were but an instant of time, we were important.

I suppose.

Moreover, as I read Facebook posts and tweets by Christians that express hatred for immigrants and minorities; as I listen to various Christian preachers insist that the conservative Republican perspective is the only political position congruent with the Bible; as I hear some Christians insist that the bombing of Hiroshima was God's will; as I hear other Christians continue to repeat the tired (and unscriptural) shibboleth that, "God helps those who help themselves" or Jesus' words that, "The poor will always be with us" to oppose any governmental help for the poor; and so on, I frequently wonder whether I would not be better off embracing Kafka's conclusion. If Christians cannot agree on what is morally right and proper, why should I believe that there is truth about anything? Cannot I just draw a page from postmodernity and adjudicate individual and corporate moral choices on the basis of social and cultural consensus? Times change, we change, morality changes. This seems perfectly sensible. It simply recognizes the reality of evolving human thought. Perhaps I'm wrong, eternally wrong, in fact, to be so absolute about my spiritual convictions.

Maybe I should be more open minded.

One of my atheist friends once suggested to me that people who believe in God are suffering from a delusion. Given the theological vagaries I mention in the last paragraph, he may well be right: if Jesus is the only way, why do Christians posit so many lenses through which to view this way? Perhaps all Christians are indeed laboring under a delusion, a delusion of their own making. Though it is a delusion that may have changed their life, it is nonetheless a delusion: how do they know it's really true?

Fair enough. Yet it's difficult to believe that over two and a half billion people, the number of people on this planet who, according to most sociological surveys, identify as Christians, are *all* suffering from a delusion. It strains credulity. There must be something more, another layer, another dimension, to the life transformation that Christianity, according to Christians, sparks in those who believe.

Unfortunately, this doesn't resolve the issues of multiple interpretations of the biblical text or what I consider to be the rabid behavior of some Christians in the public arena. We are left to ponder, again, precisely how God's music plays.

It's a slippery boundary. Though I believe God's music is always playing, I would be hard pressed to explain how, in every circumstance, it does. Even if I allow for the role of human circumstance and diversity in shaping the contours of individual belief, I am still left to wonder why the music frequently seems to play so differently from believer to believer. There is, I think, a profoundly harsh dividing line at work here. Profound because it ventures into matters ethereal and transcendent, matters that appear to be, at first glance, disquietingly malleable and flexible to interpretation; harsh in that it reduces the faith experience to a simple (dare I say simplistic?) black and white equation. To wit, God's music may play, but we struggle mightily to discern, and believe, how it does. We solve nothing.

A few years ago, I attended a reunion of some college friends. I had not seen some of them in over forty years. It was an amazing time, remarkable in every way. I'm still asking myself whether it really happened, so amazing it was. We laughed, we remembered; we talked, we conversed. As we did in college, we played loud music and danced. And of course we talked about our children.

Although thanks to Facebook and email I had re-established contact with these dear people some years ago and had shared a bit of my life with them, I had generally omitted the details of the transforming spiritual experience of which I spoke earlier. I teach theology, I wrote to them, and left it at that. Now, however, I could talk about it directly.

On Saturday morning (after staying up to the wee hours watching "Celebration," a video of Led Zeppelin's 2007 reunion concert), some of us drove to Harland and Anna-Marie's house. Along with Jeff, his best friend from childhood and who also organized the reunion, and Jeff's wife Jill, Harland and Anna-Marie had, upon graduating from college in northern Wisconsin, moved to the warmer climes of North Carolina. Ever the music aficionado, Jeff went into audio equipment sales. Always good with his hands, Harland started a roofing and remodeling business. Both did well.

Harland and Anna-Marie live in a small house set on wooden pillars in the midst of the woods. Sitting on the deck, enjoying the April sunshine, we could hear the calls of many a bird, chirping into the brilliance of the day. We spotted a family of rabbits, busily nestling in the brush, we caught a glimpse of a deer ambling through the trees. It was a pleasant place to spend a few hours.

"Tell me about how you found Jesus, Billy," Harland asked me as I sat down in a chair. It was hardly the question I expected after forty some years! But there it was. After I shared, briefly, the details of my pivotal moment with God, then summed it up by remarking that, "I had an experience of the metaphysical," Harland looked at me with longing. "I'd like that, too," he said.

I was amazed. Is God's music really playing here? And am I not the only one who hears it?

"Do you believe in an afterlife, Billy?"

"I do."

"I wish I could. Can't all of this keep going?"

"It can," I responded, "but you need to believe in God's ability to provide it. You need to trust in the God you can't now see." Never had I imagined that I would be talking with Harland about an afterlife, that I would be listening to one of my oldest friends express his wish that he could live another day. I was thankful, however, that I was. After we talked a while longer, I promised Harland that I would send him a few of my books, along with some other thoughts, and let him read and ponder.

A few days later I got a text from Harland telling me that he had received the books and materials, and that although he "didn't know" what he would find, he would read everything. Good. I very much wanted for Harland to experience what I had.

Harland and I come from very different backgrounds. He grew up in a small town in central Wisconsin, a life of cows, cheese, and dairy farms; single street towns; and tromping down quiet country roads on cold and snow bound nights. I was reared in the oceanside suburbs of Los Angeles, surfing almost every summer day, going to all kinds of rock and roll concerts, and roaming through the Santa Monica Mountains and the glitter of Hollywood's Sunset Strip. He was raised to love the Green Bay Packers (almost *de rigueur* when one lives in Wisconsin); I absorbed an appreciation for the Bruins of UCLA (my parents were alums). And so on.

But here we were, both attuned to the notion of afterlife.

As it turned out, so were other folks in our gathering that day. Of course the easy thing to say is that, religion or not, most people want to live beyond death. Most of us would like to return for "another round," wherever it might be and whatever it might look like. Although we may acknowledge, consciously or not, Kathryn Kubler-Ross's thesis that the final stage of dying is acceptance and that we are therefore prepared to enter into death with a peculiar calm, it's fair to say that many of us nonetheless would like, in our heart of hearts, an extension. Like the singer of Traffic's long ago song "The Low Spark of High Heeled Boys," we would like another chance: one more opportunity. We would like to die and wake up, wake up to find ourselves alive once more, to once more carry on. Even if it is in another existence.

On the other hand, plenty of people I know tell me that they are very content knowing that when they die they will be no more. They do not mind that they will be gone forever; they do not long for an afterlife. This life, they've decided, is enough. And that's OK: it's reality.

The puzzle remains.

When about eleven years ago the doctor who had been treating my mother for pneumonia informed me that she was not responding to the treatment and that my siblings and I would be best served to take her home to die, I called my brother, Bob, and my two sisters, Ellen and Kathleen (I'm the oldest). Come to California now, I told them, it's time (I had already been there for over two weeks).

They did. One day, Bob and I drove east into central Los Angeles to pick up a prescription for morphine, which we had been giving Mom to keep her comfortable in her final journey. After signing multiple forms and waivers, we got a little bottle of the carefully controlled substance and turned back onto the Santa Monica Freeway for the ride home. As we wound our way through the afternoon traffic, I mentioned the notion of eternal life, of living forever. Bob's response surprised me. Although he had been an atheist for decades, he said, "The idea is appealing."

I suppose it is. Yet it's an idea whose factuality, in this life, we must accept without any physical evidence for it. We cannot believe it without letting go of immediate certainty and admitting to its opposite. To take hold of a profoundly opaque unknown. To believe in the music even if we cannot hear it playing.

It is a bleak dividing line. Rational and choice making beings we suppose ourselves to be, we don't like to be forced to make a decision without visible evidence. We don't like to concede that we must believe without seeing. Or that we cannot, in this life, figure everything out. For some of us, such thoughts tear us up: we realize that we are not necessarily who we would like to think we are. And we don't take kindly to being told to forget what we "know," and to believe in what we, at present, cannot. It's an affront to all to which we have held in our lives of Western technology.

If God is there, however, the music keeps playing.

In the summer of 2016, I spoke at a gypsy village in southern Romania. Set well apart from the urban and even rural Romanian mainstream, a tangle of thatched roofs, wooden walls, and scattered bricks, this village seemed out of another age. I saw no motor vehicles, only horse or oxen drawn carts. No mechanized farming equipment, either; seeding was done with horses and plows, and harvesting with sickles. Children ran around barefoot, regardless of the terrain, and mothers did their family's laundry in a tub or stream. The sight reminded me of my time, a few years before, in Chitipa, a tiny town in northwestern Malawi, when I spoke at a pastor's conference: poverty, poverty, and more.

Nonetheless, the twenty-first century intruded in both places. As I had when I spoke in Chitipa, I noticed a few satellite dishes, along with numerous cell phones. The former perched precariously on the Romas' tattered roofs, their grey visages sparkling in the fading sun, bringing a touch of the outside world to a people that that world had abandoned long ago. "That's how the kids learn English," Catalin, the husband of the missionary couple who was hosting us, later told me. "But many of the adults," he added, "still struggle."

Romania had come a long way, I thought, since the days of communist strongman Nicolae Ceausescu who, with his wife Elena, was executed by a "court of the people" on Christmas Day in 1989. According to Catalin, Ceausescu limited the airing of cartoons (always American) to an hour and a half on Saturday mornings. And he filled the rest of the airtime, roughly three hours every night, Catalin added, with his dictatorial propaganda.

The countryside in which this village sat was beautiful, a lilting landscape of dense forest, bucolic pastures, and rolling hills. It wasn't difficult to see how the Roma would, all things considered, prefer it to life in Bucharest. "No else goes to the gypsies," Catalin noted, "but we believe they need God as much as anyone. Yes, they smell, and yes, they are sloppy, but God loves them deeply."

"Besides," Andrada, his wife, added, "the kids are so cute: I'd love to take one home!" (Catalin and Andrada had just learned that they could unfortunately not have children.)

When, earlier in the day, Catalin invited me to speak at the village that night, I had to think about what I would say. I knew no one wanted a theology lesson. Nor did anyone want an expository sermon. What about a story? So I gave a brief account of my spiritual journey. Much aware that the world out of which I had come was, literally and figuratively, eons apart from theirs, I knew I would need to contextualize my telling. I had to somehow fit my tale into their world. Per Catalin, I knew that some in my audience believed in Jesus. But many did not.

Having spent the previous four or five days studying a Romanian Bible, I had to come to know a number of Romanian words. I started by saying that I had been on a journey. When I heard Catalin say, the word, "calatorie" (journey), I saw eyes light with recognition. Aren't we all on a journey?

Then I talked about abundance. Throughout my journey I said, I sought abundance. I wanted more out of life than what I then had. And, I added, I found it. I found abundance and new life. "Abundenta," Catalin translated, he found "abundenta." And "viata": life! With this, smiles broke out, and heads nodded with understanding. Everyone, believer or not, seemed to be connecting. Somehow, I liked to think, somehow everyone heard the music playing. Somehow, everyone heard a call.

As I finished up, I said, "You must believe this for it to be true. You must take hold of it for yourself. You must leave your old journey, your old "calatorie" behind. For 'abundenta,' for 'viata,' for life and abundance."

"You must 'crede.' You must believe."

A few faces changed. Some sets of eyes dropped. Wow, wow, I thought: the dark light of faith. It's as hard to believe as it is to not.

As I noted earlier, how a person is raised or what a person experiences in her childhood can significantly, perhaps decisively, shape how this person responds to spiritual longings and leanings. As to how this happens, however, we will likely never be able to measure fully. On the other hand, it's disingenuous to say that the Roma whose eyes lit up when I mentioned life and abundance had somehow been conditioned, culturally or otherwise, to accept spirituality, or that everyone in the audience had been encouraged, surreptitiously or overtly, to believe. We still know very little about the precise relationship between heart and brain.

For I am well aware that although I once ignored the music, I now eagerly embrace it. I am equally aware that some of my oldest and dearest friends from my days of yore, my wild and wooly days prior to belief, many of whom grew up in religious households and who surely heard, in some fashion, the music, now refuse to acknowledge its existence. Furthermore, I realize that some people who were raised with no religion at all reject it until their dying day and others, like one of my nephews (one of Bob's sons), eventually come to fervently welcome it.

There are no ready answers. My siblings and I grew up in the ways and mores of the Roman Catholic Church. Catholic from the day she was born, my mother took us to mass and confession every week, shepherded us as we took our first communion, and supported us into our vows of confirmation. (Although as far as I know my father was steadfastly agnostic about religion and God until the day he died, he did not object to my mother involving their children in such things, and supported us as we went through our various rites of passage.) One could therefore argue that I was predisposed, culturally, sociologically, and otherwise, to believe in God.

Maybe. Yet at the age of fifteen, I came to reject the idea of God altogether. Seven or so years later, however, I decided to wholeheartedly accept it. Had I never really stopped believing? Had I heard but stopped listening?

To the first, absolutely not. To the second, I can only say that I'll never grasp everything that is in my heart. I'll never unpack all the epistemological and emotional dimensions of my deepest inner being. Nor will I ever fully unravel the countless tendrils of philosophical and religious perspective that have wormed their way into my life. Never.

I'm left with mystery. And God.

At a conference on the Danish philosopher Soren Kierkegaard at Baylor University which I attended some years ago, a professor of philosophy was asked why atheists do not believe in God. "They do," he replied. "They just don't know it." That some in the audience viewed his observation with skepticism didn't surprise me. After all, how can a person who disbelieves in God somehow actually believe in God? It's not logical.[2]

From the standpoint of the ubiquity of God's music, however, this speaker's contention made perfect sense. If God is there, his music must be there, too. Even, I add, issues of predestination notwithstanding, if we don't hear it.

Some years ago, I bumped into a young man on his way to the Burning Man Festival, a multi-day mélange of art, dancing, wisdom, and music held annually in the Nevada desert. I was in South Dakota at the time, doing, with a group of people from my church, a service project on the Pine Ridge Indian Reservation. He, Brent by name, was making his way from Ohio to join the Festival. I was unsure why he had routed himself through the reservation; most non-Natives, given the choice, try to avoid it. He never said, only that he just happened to be there. He apparently stumbled upon our encampment, our tents and vehicles spread out on the grounds of a decaying Episcopal church, as he drove south from Rapid City.

As Brent and I talked, it became clear to me that even though he didn't appear to have any use for conventional religion, Christianity in particular, he had decided to journey to the Festival because he had "to find my spiritual roots." Although he wasn't sure what those roots were, he was pretty much convinced that the Festival was the place to look

---

[2] And yes, I am well aware of the argument, a not terribly persuasive argument, that in disbelieving in God a person is actually affirming God's existence: why would this person not believe unless there was something in which not to believe? This is in part why the most radical atheism doesn't just disbelieve in God; it deems the very word "God" entirely devoid of content and therefore not even fitting to discuss.

for them. He was persuaded that amidst the cacophony of cultural expressions he would see there, he would eventually step into a place, a place of spirit, however he defined it, he had not been before.

As Brent and I talked that June afternoon in the Dakotas, an afternoon that, spinning out just prior to the solstice, seemed endless, the sun not being in any hurry to slip behind the grassy hills rising to the west, I thought often about the opening pages of James Joyce's *Portrait of the Artist as a Young Man*. Brent seemed a mirror of the young man Joyce so insightfully describes, a person alone and apart, untrammeled and free, someone standing on the cusp of his destiny, poised to find his path forward. Rather like, I mused, German painter Casper David Friedrich's "Wanderer above the Sea of Fog": poised on the edge of his calling.

All too similar to the me of many years before.

I did my best to explain my spiritual positions in as a non-theological way as I could. But Brent responded repeatedly that my words didn't resonate with him. He also made clear, however, that he had definitely heard a call, a deeply compelling internal directive to find himself. He had, I might suggest, heard the music. He had sensed the presence and possibility of something bigger than he, something about which he wanted to learn more. But he didn't want to learn about it in the framework of the Christian God.

I suppose I should have been disappointed that Brent didn't come to believe in Jesus. On the other hand, I suppose not. He had heard the music. His larger issue was the idea that the Christian God must be the only music. He could not abide that the Christian God is the only arbiter of spiritual truth.

That is the puzzle, I thought as I bid Brent farewell, the exasperating puzzle of faith. I can't necessarily live with it, yet I definitely can't live without it. As Sherrill had done some twenty years before, Brent had hit a nerve.

I often shudder at the exclusivity of the Christian perspective: there is no middle ground.

Moreover, I think about Proverbs 16:4, which seems to say that God chooses some people for bliss and others for destruction. What kind of a deity is he? It's too facile to say that, in essence, God is God, and we ought not to question him, or that, to use the fifty-fifth chapter of Isaiah, God's ways are not our ways. While I do not question the veracity of either position, I'm not fully convinced that, from a logical standpoint, they are not enmeshed in circularity.

Sometimes I'm not sure. Sometimes, although I unreservedly believe that God is love, I have difficulty reconciling the fact of this love with his choosing. For instance, I love my children more than other peoples' children; after all, they are mine. I saw them being born, I raised them, I know them well. Did I choose them? Did I choose for them to be born? I chose to have children, yes, but I did not choose to have the particular children I have. But I love them dearly.

On the other hand, God, if we assume him to be, as the apostle Paul, quoting one of the Greek poets of his day, described him, the one who "gives to all people life and breath and being" (Acts 17:28), it follows that everyone is, to some extent, "chosen" by God to live on this planet. That is, no one would be alive if God had not given her "breath" to be so.[3]

However, although the Bible tells us that this God is love (1 John 4:8), it also tells us that only some people are God's children (see John 1:12-13) and that, to return to Proverbs 16:4, God "has made the wicked [another word not always easy to define] for the day of evil (destruction)." Furthermore, Jesus makes clear that the road to heaven is "narrow," and that although everyone is trying to get into the kingdom of God, not everyone will (see Matthew 7:13 and Matthew 25). On the other hand, as he is hanging on the cross, his arms and legs nailed to two planks of cold rough wood, Jesus asks God on behalf of the soldiers who crucified him, "Forgive them, Father, for they do not know what they are doing" (Luke 23:34). And writing to the church at Rome, Paul tells his readers that the gift of salvation will abound to "the many" (Romans 5:15).

Clearly, however, not everyone will accept the music of God: we human beings are incredibly diverse entities. And if people do not accept the music, is this because of who they are, who they have made themselves to be, that is, the inevitable end result of their upbringing (which they did not choose), and subsequent aspirations, choices, and circumstances which they, in part, chose? Or more darkly, is it because even though God loves them, he did not oversee their entrance into this world with the intention of calling them to spend eternity with him? Or, even harder, "both and"?

---

[3] All scripture is taken from the New American Standard Bible®. Copyright ©1960, 1962, 1963, 1968, 1971, 1972, 1975, 1977, 1995 by the Lockman Foundation. Used by permission.

It's complicated.

A few years ago, I read a book (*Life's Work*) by a gynecologist named Willie Parker. Dr. Parker is a committed Christian. He was raised in the church and will believe in Jesus until his life's end. His faith and trust in God are beyond question.

Dr. Parker also does abortions. To many Christians, this raises a big "huh"? Why is a Christian doing abortions? For Dr. Parker, however, it is a matter of a woman's health and wellbeing. He does not wish to see a woman die from a "back alley" abortion, nor does he want for a woman to have to deal with a pregnancy that is the result of rape or incest. And he does not wish for a woman who, as a single mother, already has, in his (and her) view, more children than she can handle.

In the closing chapter of his book, Dr. Parker writes passionately of how he has tried to reconcile his work with the action and activity of God. God is working in the world, he says, but so are we. And we rarely know what either means fully. Because we humans can give birth to other human beings, however, we participate directly in the creative processes of the planet. We are creatures of agency, we are beings of choice.

And God, he concludes, has called us to make a choice to take care of each other.

You may agree with Dr. Parker's position, you may not. Nonetheless, his words raise intriguing questions about how we believe in the music.

And truth.

I've known Joanne since childhood: she was one of my sister Ellen's best friends. Though our life trajectories subsequently pushed us in many different directions, we, happily enough, reconnected in seminary. Like most of the women I knew in seminary, Joanne felt called to the ministry. She believed that God's music for her was, in addition to a salvific encounter with Jesus, her ordination and working as a pastor in a local church. And she held to her hearing of this music even at a time when many Christian denominations and traditions frowned upon the idea of women going into the pastorate. Even though many theologians, almost all men (although many women agreed with them), decried the thought of women entering pastoral ministry, Joanne was convinced that God was calling her to do exactly that. Things worked out for her, too: when she finished seminary, she was called to pastor a church. Later, she officiated at her father's second marriage (his first wife, Joanne's mother, died when Joanne was a little girl).

Again, if I believe in the fact of God's music, if I believe that the scriptures are to be mediated through the lens of not only the culture in which they were written but the culture in which we interpret them, I am reluctant to summarily question how another might hear it. God made us all uniquely; it follows that we will all experience him in unique ways, too.

Up to a point, of course. If Joanne had told me that she no longer believed that Jesus was God and that therefore anything he said or prescribed is not necessarily binding on us today, well, I might have had a different reaction. It's one thing to deny the core tenets of Christianity; it's quite another to dismiss what appears to be, from many standpoints, a social convention.

But let's not confuse the forest and the trees. The central

point is that God's music is playing. That is by far the most important thing. A personal transcendence is speaking. And we hear him. The immensely complex riddle embedded in this assertion, an assertion that tugs at the heart of my dilemma, however, is that we, being made uniquely in the image of God, will all grasp it differently. That it is up to us, we human beings, in all our complicated nexuses of upbringing, cultural influences, and constantly evolving experiences, to understand and accept that everyone, everyone in the uniqueness of who she is, will find her own way.

Even as the final decision is God's. My faith therefore invites me to wrestle with, wrestle with perhaps for the remainder of my days, this irresolvable tension between my limited humanity and an infinite God. As I should. A faith that cannot be questioned is not a faith worth having. By its very nature, faith demands questions. In asking me to accept the presence and truth of the unseen, to embrace a fact whose fullness is not immediately available to me, faith cannot help but be afflicted by doubt. Skepticism and query are inevitable.

This is as it should be, too. So long as I do not flatten faith altogether. If faith is infinitely malleable, forever lacking an anchor, it is not worth having.

But this creates more problems. One of the contemporary "Christian" songs that moves me most deeply is a lovely piece of poetry named "Come to the Waters." I first heard it many decades ago, during a summer, a summer barely one year removed from my turn to Jesus, in which I worked as a counselor at a Christian summer camp outside of Tyler, Texas. Had I worked as a counselor before? Absolutely not.

Did I know anything about working with eight year olds? Not at all. But in the gradual unwinding of a story which I will relate more fully later, I had recently resigned my position with a community action agency, and really needed a job. A person on camp staff who had come to town to speak at a local church mentioned, in passing, that the camp was looking for counselors for the upcoming summer season.

When I look back on this today, I chuckle at how little I knew about the faith into which I had so recently come. One of the questions on the application was, "Do you consider yourself to be an evangelical Christian?" In light of my conversion experience, I was pretty sure I was a Christian. But what did "evangelical" mean? I really didn't know. After reflecting briefly on my fading remembrances of my Catholic upbringing, I concluded that a word like "evangelical," just by the sound of it, seemed, as much I could understand the contents of words like pious or holy, to reflect such things. I answered "yes."

In "Come to the Waters," writer Marsha Stevens paints a beautiful picture of God's pursuit of us. She presents God as a being who will never stop looking for us, a person who will never stop calling us to him. Come to the waters, she pictures Jesus singing, come and be with me. Come and immerse yourself in my waters, my waters of unfathomable joy and abiding peace, and stand by my side. Enjoy me! And when you have reached the end of your earthly journey, he goes on to say, I'll welcome you to heaven's shore.

Surreal? Perhaps. But it has always tugged at my heart. When one week I took a break from counseling to oversee the camp's kitchen and was no longer responsible for eight kids twenty-four hours a day, I spent some of my afternoons (the "golden" hours between lunch clean up and dinner preparation) hiking through the periphery of the camp. Alone and relatively free, I explored some rarely used paths in the surrounding forests and hills, feeling as if I was in another world: camp seemed very far away. I admired the lakes, I touched the trees. Most of all, I gazed upward, taking in the sky. Looming over everything earthly, massive cumulus clouds scudded steadily across the pale blue firmament, rolling, turning, wrapping themselves in wave upon wave of white vapor under the burning East Texas sun. In my young Christian imagination, brimming with the words of Stevens's song, the clouds seemed a vision of heaven, windows into celestial majesty, a clarion call from God to come, to let myself fall into the arms of an eternal grace.

It was a music I had found nowhere else.

A decade or so after the enormous success of "Come to the Waters," Ms. Stevens announced that although she still believed in Jesus fervently and would proclaim her love for him to the day she died, she was, in truth, a lesbian. It was, she added, who and what God had made her to be.

For some, these were fightin' words. Lesbian? Evangelical? Impossible! Ms. Stevens's audience shrank dramatically. But like Joanne, Ms. Stevens was convinced that she was doing exactly what God wanted her to do. God had made her to be who she is. Just like he had made everyone else to be just as she is.

And Ms. Stevens is still singing. She is still singing of her love for God.

She still hears the music.

For better or worse, in the end, what will happen in my life is what God, broadly speaking, wants to happen. Likewise for Marsha Stevens. Yet I struggle to understand what our sexual inclinations mean in a world made, ordained, and purposed by an omnipotent God. We are not robots, nor are we pawns. We make choices. But so does God.

It's hard. God asks me to trust him, to trust him implicitly. Yet I'll never be able to do so in perfect light. I'll never see, fully; I'll never understand, in this life, the entire meaning of my trust. I'm trusting a being who holds all the cards in the deck. In the dark.

But isn't this the point? If God is God, well, he should have absolute power to do what he wants. It's his world, it's his cosmos. He made it, he makes the rules for it. God is the "decider." In other words, although I and God are free to choose, God is more free than I to do so.

Really? This seems to reduce me to a pawn of the infinite. I wish I could give a good reason, other than God's sovereignty and power, to justify or explain him and us. I really wish I understood. I believe in God, but I'm highly sympathetic to those who do not. At times, it does not seem to make sense.

Maybe that's why I continue to believe. Although I can't live with God, I can't live without him, either.

Midway through the eleventh chapter of John, we read that Jesus receives a message from his good friends Mary and Martha, who live in Bethany, a number of miles away. Oh, Jesus, the message goes, our brother, and your friend, Lazarus, is dying. Would you come?

For reasons the narrative does not immediately say,

Jesus doesn't go right away. He tarries. Several days later, he and his disciples appear on the outskirts of Bethany. Led by Martha, the villagers flock to Jesus, desperately milling around his little entourage. "If you had been here, Lord," Martha says, "my brother would not have died."

"Your brother will rise again," Jesus replies.

When Martha responds that, yes, she realizes that Lazarus will rise on "the last day" (the then Jewish belief that believers will be raised at the end of the age), Jesus answers in a way she could not have expected.

"I am the resurrection and the life," he says, "he who believes in me will live even if he dies. And everyone who lives and believes in me will never die." Resurrection, Jesus makes clear, is not in the future. It is now.

Jesus then asks the crowd to direct him to Lazarus's tomb. As he makes his way through the people, the text tells us, Jesus was "deeply moved in spirit and troubled." If we examine these verbs in the original Greek, we see them pointing to a profoundly visceral grief, a deep, deep moaning: a lamenting that dug to the innermost recesses of Jesus' soul. It was an ache and emptiness that split his heart apart. He couldn't bear to see such pain. Although Jesus knew that death was the inexorable lot of every human being, he hated it. He hated that death was the only way out of this existence.

Jesus then raised Lazarus from the dead.

When I therefore consider faith, life, and death together, I often recoil at the gridlock I encounter. God happens, death happens. Yet life happens, too, and a life beyond it as well. Until I die, however, I will not see them meet. Faith's brightest light is its deepest darkness

Many years ago, when my daughter Megan was eighteen, finishing up her senior year of high school, and looking forward to starting college the following August, we noticed some dramatic changes in her physical appearance. Her weight declined rapidly, she was falling asleep in every class, and her mental acuity, particularly in mathematics, had diminished greatly. However, as she had always struggled with her weight, was under considerable stress and very busy and, like everyone, had her intellectual ups and downs, we didn't think too much about it. But we did wonder what was happening.

In early July, after Megan had graduated and we had taken ourselves on a graduation trip to Jamaica (at her request), my son Payson and I took, as we had been doing for a number of years, a backpacking trip. While we had heretofore kept ourselves in the Midwest, where the hills were small and the trails short (he took his first trip when he was only ten), this time we did the "big leagues": the Rocky Mountains. We took a five night trip into the heart of the Colorado Rockies. After entering the backcountry at the Bear Creek trailhead in Rocky Mountain National Park, we hiked over the Continental Divide. Subsequently, after enjoying the "lowlands" (7,000 to 8,000 feet) for a couple of nights, we went up the other side of the divide to return to, eventually, our starting point. Aside from a brief afternoon storm our first day out, we had excellent weather. Wildlife was abundant, too: elk, sheep, deer, even a porcupine. Moreover, although Payson struggled greatly our first day on the trail, by the day we hiked out, he was bounding across the divide, reveling in the peaks spreading across it, loving the deep blue sky, and constantly telling me that, "I'm so happy!" All in all, it was a fabulous trip.

We got into O'Hare International Airport around eight o'clock in the evening. As Carol, who had picked us up, drove us home, she dropped the bombshell: Megan had cancer. How? In our absence, Carol who, even before I left, had grown very concerned about Megan's persistent cough, had taken her to a doctor. Thinking it was just a routine vascular ailment, the doctor gave Megan a prescription and sent her home. The coughing, however, didn't stop. When they made a return visit, the doctor, telling Carol that, "Now I'm looking for something," did an X-ray. The radiologist found a massive tumor in Megan's chest.

It seemed like a dream, something that couldn't really be happening. But when we arrived at the hospital from the airport and I saw Megan in a hospital bed, a red hole in her chest from a biopsy, her face sallow and weak, I no longer felt that way. Her disease was very real, far more real than I wanted it to be. Although one of my uncles, perhaps my favorite one, had died from cancer in the Eighties, and I mourned over his passing, I could not connect with the idea as fully as could his family, my aunt and cousins. Now, however, I could, in spades. I cried when I saw Megan in the bed, I cried when we had to leave her to go home. I cried that night. I cried the next day, too. And I cried before we made our first visit to an oncologist. I was overwhelmed.

God or not, hearing about the possible passing of one of my children was unspeakably jarring news.

Yet when I shared my ill fortune with a good friend, he remarked that, "Your faith will keep you." I suppose so. Hadn't it to this point? But I wondered how I was to measure the meaning of "keep"? As presence? Sustainer? Guide? Cure? Even with my faith in my heart, I had no guarantees. God is there, yes, loving, pervasive, and true. But I, and Megan are finite.

The boundary is piercing.

In informing my siblings, none of whom, as I have already noted in part, share my religious convictions, about Megan, I ended my email by saying, in a rather theologically indirect way, "In times like these, I'm thankful for the presence of larger realities in our experience, that purpose somehow remains."

It's a broken world. God or no God, I cannot expect a life absent of all pain and sorrow. Darkness hits all of us. Tragedy leaves no one out. And God's presence will not change this. God's mission isn't to prevent all pain or to stop all suffering before it happens. He will not fill all the world's cracks, he will not heal all of its fractures. He will not stand in the way of how the planet, in all its joyous and bewildering bumps, stumbles, and contusions, wishes itself to be.

God will not, in this life, undo all the effects of sin.

I will never understand why Megan developed cancer. I'll never understand why she and not one of her classmates developed a life-threatening disease. I'll never know all the contours and ramifications of what this moment in our lives meant.

Faith, however, says that, in the big picture, this is not the most important thing. What most matters, faith says, is that I trust. That I trust God regardless of the situation, and regardless of what I might want his truth to be. Because God is good.

It's powerfully wonderful. It is also highly debilitating

"This cancer is very curable," the oncologist told us when we met with him for the first time. It seems, he went on to say, to affect women at, curiously enough, either the age of eighteen or fifty. And, he added, we don't know why. He then noted that all of his patients who developed this cancer when they were in their late teens are now well into their thirties. They are married and having babies, and in every way appear as though they were never sick.

I wanted to be encouraged. I wanted this to be true. I wanted for the regime of chemotherapy which the doctor was prescribing for Megan to work, to work even better than anyone could imagine. I wanted to think there was hope. I wanted to believe that good would prevail.

Once we got home, we began calling friends, friends near and far. We asked them to pray. We asked them to call out to God for victory in this matter, to join us in petitioning God. In no time at all, prayer "chains" for Megan appeared. We began to get cards and phone calls from everyone we knew, cards and calls of encouragement, sympathy, and support. Everyone lined up behind us.

If the doctor said this cancer was eminently curable, however, why did we think we needed to pray? Was it for "insurance"? Was it so that we could feel the care of others? Was it because we thought, consciously or not, that the more people who prayed, the more likely it was that Megan would be cured?

All of these thoughts ran through our minds, constantly. In the end, however, we prayed because we really did believe that there were "larger presences" in our reality, larger presences that, however bewildering they can sometimes be, ensured purpose. Yet we also believed that this purpose is not one of cause, nor is it one of reason. And it's not a purpose in which all questions are answered and all queries find explanation. It is rather a purpose that announces and demonstrates the fundamental intelligibility and meaningfulness of this existence. It is the purpose of an intentionally created universe. We are not accidents.

After four months, two months before she was scheduled to finish her chemotherapy, Megan did not display any signs of cancer. She appeared to be fully "cured." We were grateful, incredibly grateful. We were grateful for our friends, we were grateful for modern medicine, we were grateful to God. He had "come through."

So it seemed. But that's not the point. Faith isn't about what does or does not happen. It's about trust. To live with faith is to live on the edge of rationale and reason. It is to agree that although purpose is pervasive and omnipresent, it is a purpose which we rarely see in full. Faith balances the light of the music with the darkness of existence, all the while never knowing, precisely, how these meet.

It's a wild hope.

But faith cannot be any other way. It must be a wild hope, it must be a hope unseen. That's its foolishness, that's its wisdom.

It's as awesome as it is vexing.

Many decades ago, shortly after my father died (a story which I will recount in greater detail later), after I had returned to Illinois from my parents' home in Los Angeles, and I was reflecting, once more, on the enormity of my loss, I put on an album of the Romanian pianist Dinu Lipatti. As the needle steadily made its way across the grooves of black vinyl, finally to land on Johann Sebastian Bach's "Jesu, Joy of Man's Desire," I wept. Not many years before, I had played this album for Dad. He and Mom had invited me for dinner (I was in seminary at the time, living about fifteen miles away), and I had just bought the album. As the opening chords of "Jesu" entered the room, Dad exclaimed, "That's Bach!"

For one moment, one achingly brief moment in the gloomy afternoon of a Chicago winter, I felt, felt almost instinctively, the purpose: God's purpose. I felt as if everything had been resolved, as if everything had been restored. Only, however, if I believed it. Transcendence's ineffability is its own sublimity. Only faith can see it.

A little over a year into my Christian journey, I saw a college friend at a job orientation session in, of all places, Dallas, Texas. I had not seen Fred in four years. When we knew each other in San Francisco (when we attended San Francisco State University), we knew no boundaries. Here we were, two people newly liberated from parental constraint, two affluent young white people who, due to circumstances which neither of us could have predicted, found ourselves in a cultural miasma of mind boggling proportion. As if we had awoken from a dream and were still rubbing our eyes, trying to adjust to what turned out to be an insidiously deceptive light. Plato's cave it was not.

For nearly two years, Fred and I went wild together, laughing madly at all things conventional, running insanely through each day before us, always celebrating the joy of limitless mayhem and mirth. Always, always, we dared the world, the indefinable world of the "establishment," to come after us, to hunt us down for our perfidy. Over and over, we skewered everything that we believed our elders deemed socially acceptable. We wouldn't listen to anyone.

Fast forward to the other side. Not that I was any more willing to listen to anyone now, but that I was certainly willing to listen to God. Fred was not. "What happened to you?" he said. "Did you find Jesus?" And he laughed. Once, we had laughed together. Now, one of us was laughing at the other.

But I was laughing, too. I was laughing at the incongruity of who I now was, the striking mismatch between the past and present. Once I laughed at what I knew; now I laughed at what I did not.

Yet other than telling Fred the story of how I came to believe or sharing my nascent grasp of theological dogma with him, I could say very little to him about what had happened. I knew what I had found, but I also knew that I could not easily explain it. Once Jesus had annoyed me. Now he thrilled me. How could I rationally describe what I scarcely knew myself?

At this point, all I really knew was that, to enlarge on that to which I have already alluded, on an October night along Jasper's Athabasca River, I decided that Jesus promised me a life more abundant than anything I had experienced before. That when I said "yes" to Jesus, when I decided to call his name into the darkness of the forest in which I was standing, I would find an abundance far surpassing anything else I had known.

And I did. In an instant, everything changed. In the sweep of a moment, I felt as if all my angst had been resolved, and my every emptiness had been filled. I felt flooded with purpose, overwhelmed with point. Everything seemed to come together. I felt reborn.

When I tried to communicate this to Fred, well, things did not go swimmingly. "Born again?" he smirked, "how do you know?" He had a good point: although I knew what I knew, I didn't know it enough to know it all.

When I saw Fred the next day, he sniggered at me again. "How can you believe this stuff?"

As I will say repeatedly in this meditation, faith is just that: faith. I believe in a mystery or, as Paul puts it in 1 Corinthians 13, "in a riddle." Not that God is beyond knowing; far from it. But that however strongly I believe, I will never know, in this life, everything about what I believe. There will always be something about faith, and God, that I will not be able to fully explain without invoking, well, faith.

It's a monstrous chasm.

Some of my atheist friends find this infuriating. "Do I truly need to be 'born again' to understand?" they often ask me. Or, "do I really need a 'special' experience to know God?"

Or the personal favorite of the "ornery" person I mentioned earlier, "Are you saying that the only way I can believe is to believe? That's illogical."

For better or worse, however, though I believe that my faith is reasonable and logical, I am also acutely aware that getting to this faith may well require one to suspend her loyalty to the epistemological supremacy of both. It's not easy.

Particularly if I contend that the music is always playing. Well before her first birthday, we bought a little book for Megan at the Moody Bible Institute's bookstore in Chicago.

Its title was *God is with Me*. Adapted from the text of Psalm 139, it communicates, over and over, that wherever we go or whatever we do, God is with us. Always. Always, always, and always, God is with us.

Megan was quite taken with this book. She wanted it read to her constantly, and took it everywhere she went. Even to the island of Kauai in Hawaii. The consulting firm for which Carol worked, and in which she eventually became a managing principal, sold benefit plans, funded by life insurance, to corporations. This required the firm to work with insurance companies. Such companies customarily "reward" their best sellers with "special" trips. One year, Carol's firm was given some slots on a trip to Kauai. Because she was so young, we took Megan with us. Megan spent most of the eight hour airplane flight walking up and down the aisles of the jumbo jet in which we were traveling. She didn't sleep a wink. Nor did we!

One morning in our hotel room, as Carol and I were talking in our bed, Megan began to stir and, within seconds, bolted awake in the roller bed in which we had put her. The first thing she did was to grab and hold up *God is with Me*: it was time to read!

However, was it our music or God's?

A few nights after I was told that Jesus offered me a more abundant life, I was browsing the books in Jasper's tiny town library. On a lark, I pulled a black book titled *Jesus* off the shelf and, barely thinking about it, started reading. Without knowing it at the time, I came upon John's account of Jesus' raising of Lazarus (which I mentioned a number of pages ago). As you may recall, as John relates the episode, Jesus remarks that those who believe in him will "live forever."

To my surprise, I found myself singularly captivated by this promise. I immediately set the book down and strode out of the library. All I could think about was wow: abundant life, forever. Eternal purpose, eternality of person. What could be finer?

Endless communion with God: God always with me, now and forever.

So I thought. Nonetheless, it's a delicate balance. Because I had already come to believe in Jesus, I was much more inclined to believe his words to be true. Yet I could not have believed unless I had been willing to deny, a few nights before, that I could know *more* than what I believed. I had to make faith the ground *and* the sustainer of my knowing. I had to pit not knowing against knowing, and conclude that, in the big picture, it is better for me to abjure knowing than to insist that I can.

The paradox often terrifies me.

Yet even in this early part of my faith journey, I usually thought far more about having abundance and presence in this life than abundance and presence in the next. Despite how its promise catapulted me to faith that night in Jasper, I don't think much about the idea of eternal life today. Some might find this odd, which is fine. But it is why as I considered how to explicate to Fred the nature of my faith, I focused on the notion of present meaning. Even though I had once felt the idea of eternality in a highly forceful way, today I wasn't necessarily looking for its fulfillment. I wasn't really looking for a "pie" in the sky. I was looking for a "pie" in the here and now.

Hence, after Fred asked me why I believed in "this stuff," I told him that I didn't believe because one day I will see God. I believe because I believe I can experience God now. I can have abundance today. Let the afterlife, I added, take care of itself. I know it's there, but I don't want to live my life longing for it.

"Good," he replied, "eternal life is foolishness. How can anyone believe that one day they will live forever? It's delusional."

It was hard to argue his point. Sometimes I just don't know. Although an afterlife, the idea of a consciously joyous life beyond this one, looks good on paper (even, as I noted earlier, to an atheist like brother Bob), when I view it outside the lens of faith (as millions of people do), it often perplexes me. It even frightens me. How can there be a place of endless bliss? How does it work that after my years of living amidst the ruptures of this planet I will be translated and transported to another realm, a heavenly realm in which nothing will ever break again, forever and ever? Yes, it will be wonderful to see what existence really means, to see God as he really is, and to have all questions answered and all problems solved. To never have to die. And it is absolutely amazing to think that I will experience this with many of the people whom I knew in my earthy existence. It all seems so glorious.

It also seems surreal. As it should: it's not of this world. On the other hand, when I think about ideas like predestination, eternal damnation, judgment and the lake of fire, and realize that some people and things, regardless of the joy they may have brought me in my earthly life will, the other side of death, be no longer being thought of or remembered, I do wonder. I wonder how something so curiously wonderful can be so achingly dark and troubling.

They talked a lot about heaven, those Catholic nuns who taught me faithfully did, week after week, year after year, in Sunday school (which we called catechism). Although, regrettably, they told me, upon death I'd probably spend time in Purgatory, being purified from my many venial sins, eventually—and in due time—they assured me, I would be with God.

"What did this mean?" I often asked. "How will this happen?"

"I don't really know, but I do know that it will be more beautiful than you can imagine," was the frequent reply.

"But what is that like?"

"No one can say. But you'll be happier than you will ever know."

I never found this very satisfying. Growing up, our family camped every summer. For about two weeks in July or August, we packed up and drove out of Los Angeles, usually to the national parks of the Sierra Nevada. Sometimes we drove to Zion National Park in Utah, Grand Canyon National Park in Arizona, or the Grand Tetons in Wyoming. We all loved it. In our earliest years, we drove in station wagons. Mom and Dad sat in the front seat, and we four kids shared two rows of back seats. As this was in the days before seat belts, we were free to roam about these seats at will. As we grew older, we switched to sedans, which created seat problems of its own. But that's another story.

For a few years we had a Chevy station wagon called a "Clamshell Wagon," in which the far back row of seats faced the rear of the vehicle. Those who sat in it were therefore looking at what the car was leaving behind. When the car stopped, they stared into the faces of the drivers of the car behind us. Slightly awkward, yes, but we didn't care. Besides, our particular model was such that we could, if we wished, fold this seat down and into the next section of seats. Then we could lie down and look out the side windows.

As I lay on these folded down seats while Dad tooled across central California to get to the Sierra, I often focused not on the land but the sky. I looked at the clouds, the massive cumulus formations floating lazily across the blue. They were always shifting, always changing, always becoming something new. What if these clouds, these enormous puffs of white, I often thought, were heaven? And what if God was moving these clouds to prepare places for everyone? What if this constantly changing panorama of skyward wonder was my future home?

Nonetheless, it was hard to see the point.

As it is today. As much as I wrestle with all the ramifications of eternal life, however, I also realize that I cannot predict how I will feel on my death bed, provided I am fortunate enough to consciously experience it. I cannot know, now, how I will go into my passing. I don't know whether I will cower in fright, laugh out loud, or weep uncontrollably. Or something else.

I also don't know whether I will be disappointed when I step into the other side. In this life, I'm still dangling between knowing and not.

After he announced, in 2004, that he had come to believe in God, renowned British philosopher and once stalwart atheist Anthony Flew remarked in an interview that he didn't think he would want to live forever. Though he affirmed, in logical and philosophical principle, the idea of God, he was reluctant to invest it with the possibility of eternal bliss. What, to him, would be the point? Isn't it enough to agree that we cannot understand reality without the notion of God?

On the one hand, I concur totally. If the afterlife is as the Bible describes it, a heavenly city with walls of precious gems and streets of golden glass, I need to say that it appears to be endorsing some of the transient pleasures of present society. Rather than tone down materiality, it seems to accentuate it. It makes me wonder why Christianity, a religion that encourages people to hold loosely the things of this life, appears to embed its afterlife with the furtive glitter of this earthly existence.

Also, knowing that in responding to a question about heaven, Jesus replies, as Luke's gospel records it, "In the resurrection, you will not be giving and taking in marriage," complicates matters for me further. Will Carol and I not be together?

More importantly, I wonder what we will do in heaven: just hang out?

Perhaps the thing that troubles me most about the afterlife, however, is that for many believers, it is the primary reason why they believe. "I'm just passing through this world," they tell me. Or as a friend of mine once said in talking about the problems in his workplace, "Who cares? I'm going to heaven."

George Mallory was a British mountaineer who, in 1924, perished on the upper slopes of Mt. Everest, less than, most researchers think, 800 vertical feet from the summit. To this day debate continues over whether Mallory and his partner, Andrew Irvine, actually reached Everest's summit. This notwithstanding, Mallory is perhaps most famous for his reply to a reporter's query about why he wanted to climb Everest. "Because it's there," he said.

Indeed. I believe in Jesus, I believe in God. They're "there." And part, an integral and essential part, of them being "there," is believing that God is eternal. He has always been, he always is, and he always will be. I might say that eternal life is part of the package. If I am to believe in God, I must believe in everything that he is, his music, his Tree of Life and, crucially, his eternality and heaven. I can't have a seminal present without an equally seminal future; by its very nature, eternality holds present and future inextricably together. I can't have one without the other.

But it's more than sheer logic. Hovering in the background as I write these words is the music of Johannes Brahms's *Ein Deutsches Requiem* ("A German Requiem"). Music lovers know that despite the highly biblical lyrics he used in this piece, Brahms didn't really believe in a conventional "Christian" afterlife. In fact, he may not have believed in any afterlife at all. As a nineteenth century Romantic, Brahms believed in the power of Nature to shape and define all things. There was nothing beyond Nature. Out of Nature we come and, one day, to it we will return.

No afterlife is necessary.

For at death we are, to mention God's words at the close of novelist Jorge Borges's parable "Everything and Nothing," at once "many and [yet] no one."

Life is over.

One of the *Requiem's* choruses is, "Blessed are the Dead" (*Selig sind die* Toten). As I listen to its words, I'm reminded of the dictums in Ecclesiastes 7 that, "It is better to go to a house of mourning than a house of feasting," and "The end of a matter is better than its beginning." And the observation of chapter four, "So I congratulated the dead who are already dead more than the living who are still living." Maybe death is better. Maybe it is better that the pain and hardship that frequently intrude into this life will one day come to an end. As Aunt Patty, one of Mom's four sisters, said when Aunt Joan, her and Mom's only other living sister at the time, and long afflicted with dementia, finally passed away at the age of 90. "Her suffering is over."

If Nature is all that is, then, yes, Aunt Joan's suffering is indeed over. As is her life, forever. She is totally gone. And we are happy for her. We are happy that she is no longer in any pain. If I believe in God, however, if I believe in, as singer Joan Osborne put it, Jesus and the prophets and saints, then I must believe otherwise. I must believe in an afterlife. God, the present, and eternity are one and the same expression of existence.

Yet it's not just a matter of saying that I "must" believe. I *want* to believe in an afterlife. If God is indeed there, I want all that he is for me. Even if I have question upon question about how and why this next life will happen, questions for which I will not in this life receive answers, and even in the face of a steady and abject unknowing, I want to experience the fullness of my relationship with him.

Even if it seems no more than a trick of logic. And even

if I can't see or hear it. Sometimes faith is its own worst enemy.[4]

The book of Job, a book to which I will return repeatedly, is well known for its agonizing depiction of Job's frustration with God about human suffering. Reading it sometimes

---

[4] That said, allow me to digress a bit and say that the greater challenge for believers is understanding that agreeing to the reality of heaven does not disabuse us of full heartedly tending to the life of this existence. As Jesus, God came into this world. Born as a human being, Jesus laughed, cried, slept, got hungry, felt full, and suffered the various indignities and inconveniences of life that all of us do. Jesus' time on earth affirms the importance of our present existence. This life matters.

Furthermore, when he created the world, God called it good. Nowhere in the Bible does God call the world bad. Yes, he criticizes the many wicked deeds in which human beings engage, and yes, he repeatedly notes the evil and aberrant tendencies resident in the human heart, and, yes, he at times seems to accept, even ordain, that certain people will be so evil that they are beyond redemption. But God never says that the world is inherently bad. God loves his creation. Indeed, Romans 8 tells us that, in the end, God will redeem and restore the entire created order to its original beauty. God wants the best for the world.

And so should we. The world is our home. We are not to run away from this existence. We are to live in it, live avidly, intently, and compassionately. Believing in heaven should not change the intensity with which we live our present lives. As God, speaking through the prophet Jeremiah, tells the Jewish exiles in Babylon, "Build houses and live in them; and plant gardens and eat their produce; take wives, become fathers, and take wives for your sons and give your daughters to husbands. Seek the welfare of the city where I have sent you" (Jeremiah 29:5-7). Put another way, even if you are where you don't want to be, bloom. Bloom where God has planted you.

makes me wonder why we even summon the energy to live. At times, Job's laments really do lead me to agree with German philosopher Arthur Schopenhauer's assertions about cosmic pessimism or French writer Albert Camus's observations about life's inherent absurdity. We are born, we look for a meaning that we never find, then we die. Or as the writer of Ecclesiastes observes, "But better off than both of them [those who are living as well as those who have died] is the one who has never existed, who has never seen the evil activity that is done under the sun" (Ecclesiastes 4:3).

Absent a God, Schopenhauer, Camus, and Ecclesiastes are absolutely correct. In his memoir *The Diving Bell and the Butterfly,* Jean-Dominique Bauby tells the story of how he, once a successful fashion designer and magnate, was one day driving through the French countryside when he suffered a massive stroke. This was no ordinary stroke. It left Bauby with what is called "locked-in syndrome," a condition which rendered him unable to move more than a few parts of his forehead and his left eyelid. It was the cruelest of fates. He couldn't smile; he couldn't laugh or frown; he couldn't make a "snide" remark or humorous aside. He certainly couldn't talk. His life of freedom, wealth, and privilege was over, irreparably over.

Given his condition, Bauby could only write *Diving Bell* with the help of a therapist who assigned eye blinks to the letters of the French alphabet (each word took roughly two minutes to write). Bauby blinked, she wrote. And a masterpiece was born.

A little over a year after his diagnosis, Bauby was gone. Absurd? Not completely: Bauby left us with a remarkable record of living boldly in the face of worldly hopelessness.

Yet if I view Bauby's life through the prism of Paul Sartre's contention that humanity is no more than a "useless passion," it is. Bauby was but a random spark in an unexplainable fire. His meaning, the meaning of who he is, well, it never really was.

While I do not doubt that forty-six years of believing in Jesus has decisively shaped my thinking in this regard, I nonetheless crater at the apparent senselessness of existence in a world devoid of God. In this, Sartre was more than prescient: without a God, he observed, life indeed has absolutely no final meaning.

Even if, as almost every human being does, we try to make it otherwise. We constantly seek to affirm the glorious tragedy of human existence. What else can we do?

Once upon a time, my parents, my mother and father, were born. They grew up, they found each other, they had children, they built a life together. Then they died. And we mourned them, mourned them deeply. We still do. We mourn our father, whose death I mentioned a few pages ago, in particular. Dad died at the age of sixty-three, shocking us all, wrenching us out of the happy worlds we had so naively constructed, driving a wedge into our culturally driven expectations about human longevity. Over thirty-seven years later, we still miss him. Our mother lived on, watching us come into our adult lives, delighting as we found spouses, thankful as we had children, amazed as we moved to middle age and beyond. Mom died at the age of eighty-eight. She was a widow only six years less than she had been married to Dad. Her death was the end of our familial foundation. It left a hole we could never fill.

Yet we live on. We live on as images and mirrors of our

parents, as people whom they raised, taught, and shaped into the people we are today. Mom and Dad's lives therefore continue. And they will do so even after all of us are gone. Although our—my siblings and my—children never knew Dad, and because due to distance they saw Mom infrequently, they will nonetheless, largely unwittingly, sustain Mom and Dad's lives in turn. And so on. Who Mom and Dad were, just as who their ancestors were, will likely never perish altogether.

Yet I wonder whether this, in itself, justifies Mom and Dad's existence. I wonder whether it validates the apparent absurdity of their lives, that they were born, lived, and died, never to "be" again. I question whether it counters Job's lament that, "Man, who is born of woman, is short-lived and full of turmoil, like a flower he comes forth and withers, fleeing like a shadow, never to remain"? (Job 14:1)

On one hand, I suppose it does. I suppose that my mother and father's legacy, transmitted, in some fashion, over many generations to come, affirms the weight of their lives, and upholds the meaningfulness of their existence, apart and together. I suppose. Their lives had been worth their measure. At least as we humans like to see it.

Nonetheless, this doesn't necessarily dispel the fundamental angst of human existence. It does not remove the terminality of death, it does not take away the certainty of the fate that awaits all of us. As one who is as mortal as anyone else, I must therefore ask: is my faith, my faith in God and his greater purpose, sufficient for me to overcome this unavoidable crux of sentient existence?

I'd like to think so. But maybe not. "I'm not afraid to die," Priscilla, one of my atheist friends says often to me.

"When it's my time, I'll go. I want to live as long as I can, but I'm ready to go when it is my time." I'm not sure who or what will decide Priscilla's "time," but I find this to be as clear-eyed an acceptance of life's friability as I have heard. Many others would agree with Priscilla on this: they love living, but they're not afraid to die.

Or as Percy Shelley put it in "Adonais," his deeply moving elegy for the recently deceased John Keats, "What Adonais is, why fear we to become?"

Sometimes, however, a person does not know he is about to die. In his twentieth year, John, the older brother of one of my students from many years ago, was diagnosed with a particularly virulent form of bone cancer. His parents took him all over the country in an effort to find a cure, trying anything that would halt the disease's relentless destruction of his body. In the end, tragically, they had to make one of the hardest decisions a parent has to make. One March morning, looking at their son, their first born, now comatose, existing only through life support, his days beyond redemption, in a hospital bed in North Carolina, they called John's sister Emily, their only other child, to say, "John's not going to make it. We're pulling the plug."

We will never know exactly what John was thinking as his life force left him. Unlike many of us, alert and aware as we expire, John was likely barely aware of himself as he passed on. In the weighty swoop of an instant, everything that he had been, everything that he had done, and everything he had dreamed (he wanted to be an airline pilot), was over.

And he could see and do nothing about it.

The title of an issue of the *New York Times Magazine* that comes out every December is, "A Life Well Lived." Page after page, various writers remember the glory, greatness and, conversely, shortcomings, foibles, and tragedies, of many of the more memorable, to their minds anyway, fellow human beings who passed away that year. They highlight what these people were able to do, laud how their lives have shaped and impacted the world. They express their gratitude and pleasure that these folks lived. Their lives, they believe, counted.

Or as French poet Charles Baudelaire observed in his "The Death of the Poor," "It is Death which consoles, alas! and makes us live; it is the aim of life, the one aspiration."

Such talk, however, seems very shallow in the case of the death of an infant. Or the cold-blooded murder of a person in her thirties, a deed of suffering and pain. Or genocide. And more. Such things beg the question of life's meaning. They are holes far more difficult to fill.

I certainly do not understand the seeming randomness of life. I do not understand why some people live many years, and other people do not. And I do not comprehend why some people who do much evil (as we define such things) outlive, often by many years, those who do much good. For instance, Brunhilde Pomsel, long-time secretary to Nazi leader Joseph Goebbels, lived to the age of 106. American civil rights leader Martin Luther King died at age thirty-nine. Similarly, Nazi film maker Leni Riefenstahl lived to 101, and Pakistani leader Benazir Bhutto only 54: why?

Or why was I born white, raised in privilege and never lacking for anything, while millions of other children around the world are born and die in dismal poverty, never to see their sixth birthday? Why? Why must life be this way?

Don't tell me it's because of sin. Don't say that the

world's brokenness is not God's fault but humanity's. Do not summarily claim that God wants something better. Although I do not doubt that, for reasons I will eventually explicate, these things are true, I believe they present too cavalier a face about present tragedy. They still leave us scrambling to explain the absurdity of existence. They leave me still wondering about the meaning of faith's wild hope.

Vera had just turned ninety. She had always been healthy, strong, purposeful, getting around on her own, and living happily in the house in which she had been over sixty years. But in the space of a few weeks, in consecutive order, she fell at her home, developed pneumonia, and contracted a bacterial infection in her small intestine. Her doctors, however, remained optimistic that she would recover and be able to resume her normal activities.

All that changed in one day. One Saturday morning, barely twenty-four hours after we had paid Vera a visit in the hospital, her youngest son called us to say that she was, as the nurses had put it, "transitioning." Death was near.

A week before, in a lucid moment, Vera had shared with us, Carol and me, her fear of dying. She wanted to live. She wanted to go back to her little house. She wanted to stay in the world. But she also asserted, repeatedly, her faith in God. She was confident that when she passed, she would do so in the arms of God. She was content and, despite her very human apprehensions of leaving this life, ready to, as Christianity likes to say, "go home."

And so she did, quietly breathing her last at 10:30 a.m. on a cold and snowy day in the February of her ninetieth year. We were unbearably sad, but assured: we knew, and believed, that she was in a far better place. A place beyond our mortal imaginings. A place apart.

Absurdity was vanquished. Vanquished in the hoped for hiddenness to come.

Unfortunately, however, Vera is still dead. Her sons will never see her again. Her earthly life is a finished story. There will be no sequel. Faith, however, says there is. Faith says that there is more. Nonetheless, I still struggle to define my present connection to it, this sequel, this God's eternity, this hidden eternity into which I believe Vera has come. I'm still left to speculate about how, precisely, this eternity will eclipse all absurdity and how, precisely, it will resolve my temporal struggles and confusion.

But I believe it will.

Faith's fulcrum turns, oddly enough, on its absence of clarity. Though faith is, as its Greek roots make clear, a faith and hope of "confident expectation," it is a confident expectation whose fullest picture presently eludes me. It asserts the fact of a future I cannot presently see. The wholeness of its wonder is hidden in the shrouds of mortality. Faith shouts God in a world with no place for him.

If I am to therefore insist that faith, faith in God and his resurrection power, is sufficient for overcoming the raw physicality of death, I do so in an earthly vacuum. I cannot now see the afterlife; I cannot now see God. Despite my belief in the veracity of the biblical accounts of Jesus' resurrection, and despite my clear-eyed evidence of how his resurrection inspired and sustained the early church, its numerous martyrs in particular—and death bed conversions and so-called "near death experiences" notwithstanding—I am nevertheless left to stare into the singularly terrifying orifice of death without any present and visible evidence that it has another side. I am still standing at the most frightening and unnerving crossroads of human existence with no way forward—or back.

Bluesman Robert Johnson's crossroads it is not.

This is faith's defining assertion of itself: it sets my faith journey directly before that which ends it. Then it tells me to move right through it. t reminds me that I do this because, and only because, on the basis of my life long journey of research, thought, and prayer, I am absolutely convinced of God's presence. Absolutely and unreservedly.

It's a prospect that is at once dreadful and troubling; at once emotionally jarring and intellectually enervating. It is also a prospect that is marvelously wonderful. It is faith in its fullest possible definition: total and absolute trust.

Frankly, if God is of this life only, I don't need him. I don't need an earthly God to live and die in a finite world. No one does. God is only God if he is here *and* beyond, if he is present in the "now" as well as present beyond the now. Yes, faith doesn't always know how. That's not its point. Faith will always generate temporal tension. It must. And yes, faith doesn't know, precisely, *how* resurrection and the afterlife happen. But it believes in both. For as we shall see time and time again in the course of this narrative, we are beings who instinctively desire to connect with transcendence. We need a God who is beyond.

Even if we don't want to.

When Mom died, a story I recounted earlier, Bob, Ellen, Kathleen, and I found different ways to deal with our grief. For me, it was bible study and prayer. For Bob, ever the atheist, and despite his endorsement of the appeal of everlasting life I mentioned previously, it was a renewed and grudging acceptance of the fleetingness and mortal certainties of existence. For Ellen, it was a great deal of reflection, reflection that, like that of Bob, tried to come to grips with the pain and inevitability of death. As to Kathleen, the youngest in the family, it was a mix of present and future, a belief that Mom now inhabited a "spirit" world and that she would somehow live on.

I do not pretend to know or claim whose level of comfort was greater. But I do think that in looking to some sort of higher realm of existence and being, Kathleen and I were able to deal with our grief in a way that Bob and Ellen could not. Even if we could not see it. Bob and Ellen's was a comfort and hope of this world and this world only. It is not a comfort and hope, however, that I dismiss. Not at all. It's just that, dare I say, it misses the larger point. It misses that, without transcendence, solace and hope cannot decisively overwhelm grief. It's one part of immanence against another.

I came to realize, however, that even if, to me, my faith in God's hope provided a way (not a precise picture) to "why," it also, ironically enough, potentially compounded my grief, too. A number of years ago, I read a letter to the editor of the *New York Times* in which the writer, an avowed atheist, remarked that he was in fact envious of believers. In times of suffering, he wrote, believers can turn to God for comfort and purpose. He could not. He was left, he said, with trying to navigate the pain on his own.

But he closed his letter by stating that, nonetheless, he would rather step bravely into a void without explanation than turn to the "crutch" of belief in God.

Belief is a comfort, yes, but belief also raises questions.

While its hope answers why, it also affirms that this why is a why embedded in another realm, one of the supernatural and transcendent, one into which I cannot presently go. Hence, if in my belief, my faith, I insist that I know there is, somewhere, somehow, a why, and that I am therefore good with whatever life's circumstances bring me, I must tread carefully. I still cannot *definitively* prove it.

Except to say that otherwise I could not make sense as of myself as a human being.

For many years, during our Christmas school break, our Aunt Velma, Dad's only sister, would pick a day and take the four of us to Disneyland. We loved it. We loved getting up early and driving through the morning rush hour traffic; entering the grand entrance of the park and buying our tickets; wandering to our favorite rides; and eating snack upon snack, all the while basking in the warmth of a December sun in Los Angeles.

Whenever Dad invited Velma over for dinner, we all had a laugh. To Dad's chagrin, Velma would share part of her meal with our cat Sam as he prowled around the table. Waiting until Dad wasn't looking, she happily passed off some of her meat to him. Sam knew she was an easy mark. He also knew that Dad would fume if we tried to do the same thing. He was no dummy.

Velma looked more like my grandfather than any of her brothers (including Dad, she had three). And I loved my grandfather dearly. When I was making my initial forays into the world of protest in Sixties America, contacting the Students for a Democratic Society and requesting literature, organizing various protests around town, and calling policemen "pigs," my grandfather one day approached me and asked me a question. "Bill, I hear you're in the SDS."

Though I wasn't quite sure what he was thinking, I gingerly indicated that I was. "That's great!" he said. To this day, I still own the booklets of the sayings of Chairman Mao Zedong (at that time he was Mao Tse-tung) that he sent me. Grandpa had obtained them directly from the Chinese Communist Party's headquarters in what was then called Peking.

Dad hadn't been dead for more than three years when my siblings and I learned that Velma was in the hospital, terminally ill. It would not be long, we were told.

One day, Mom's call came. "Was anyone with her when she died?" I asked.

"Unfortunately not," Mom said. I cried. I hoped that even though she was alone, Velma had died experiencing anticipation and wonder, that she had passed into the eternity of a loving and transcendent God. Faith told me I could hope this way, yet faith also told me that, apart from knowing the spiritual inclinations of Velma's heart, inclinations which, despite much conversation I had had with her over the years, I still had not been able to pinpoint precisely, I could not.

I'm still in the darkness, the darkness of a faith whose deepest riddles evade solution. My faith is a faith in puzzlement, the puzzlement of the loving presence of God. Or as my Jewish brothers and sisters call it, the *shekinah* behind the veil: the certainty of an unseen factuality.

Barely one year after her call about Velma, Mom called with more heartbreaking news. Our Uncle Charles and Aunt Gwen, both of whom had struggled with debilitating back pain for decades, were dead. About a week prior to her call, Mom had received a letter from Gwen. After describing their sense of hopelessness regarding their pain and remarking that the time had come to end it, Gwen closed with "Farewell." Her suspicions aroused, Mom called the Nevada trailer park in which they had been living for many years.

When the trailer park manager went to check on Charles and Gwen, he came upon a gruesome scene. They were lifeless, lying in pools of their own blood. From what the police were able to piece together, it seemed that after slashing Gwen's throat, Charles proceeded to stab himself in the chest until he died. Blood was spattered all over the trailer. It was a tragic end.

Had Charles and Gwen lost hope? So it seemed. Yet were a person who trusted in Jesus to encounter such pain, what would her hope be? However much she prayed, palliative relief might never come. All she could see ahead was a lengthy and arduous journey to death. Then heaven. Is it worth it?

It's brutal. To hope in faith demands an unswerving, an absolutely unswerving trust that over and above all else, purpose is present. And that this purpose exceeds, exceeds infinitely, what is now. It is also to say to a person who has placed her trust in Jesus that the pain she is now experiencing is on the one hand entirely present and real, yet on the other hand it is the path, as horrible as it may be, to a richer life and, one day, the "greater thing" that will follow it. In addition, it is to say to her that this all hangs on her faith, her frightfully tenuous and, at times, profoundly discomfiting, faith. It's not her logic, it's not her reason. It's not even her previous experience. It's her faith: her trust in God.

I have no idea how long my earthly days will be. Moreover, I may well develop a condition whose pain will be with me the rest of my life. I might suffer every moment of every day. Nonetheless, I am, as the psalmist writes, to be confident, to be confident in the goodness of God (Psalm 27:3). I am therefore to step forth boldly, to step boldly into what lies ahead. At the same time, however, I am to wait. I am to wait for the ineffable confluence of worldly circumstance, human will, and divine purpose to definitively work itself out in my life. I am to wait for that which I cannot control, that in which I have no say.

But that in which I believe. Even in the face of intractable present agony or pain. Even though I will die.

Faith drives a grim bargain. I cannot have genuine hope without genuine faith in a genuine God; yet I cannot have genuine faith in a genuine God without a genuine hope that I will, one day, see both. It is a darkness at once foreboding and transforming, a darkness of mortality and temporal misgiving, yet a darkness of eternal light and illumination.

Present lucidity is elusive.

Decades ago, less than a year before we left Dallas for Chicago, Carol and I got a phone call from one of Carol's oldest friends. Two days earlier, as he had been running on the track at his gym, Mary Jane's husband Al had, without any warning, collapsed and died. Heart attack. He was only thirty-six years old. When a few hours later we got to their house, we saw scores of people, standing in the front yard or sitting in the living room. No one was sure what to do. Al's death was so sudden.

Both Al and Mary Jane were believers. Both believed that life did not end at death. Both believed that they would see each other again. As Mary Jane began the lengthy process of working through her grief and her children began to adjust to life without a father, I thought about this a lot. I came to realize that the shallow faith which I had held since I began my Christian journey, the faith that everything would always work out, had missed the mark. Mary Jane had just lost her life partner: faith is anything but transactional. It's trust, trust in presence, God's constant and unyielding presence.

Yet a presence I cannot see.

I met Chris when I spent a summer working in Dallas (the summer I met Carol) during my seminary days. As I had not come to Dallas with a vehicle (I flew out from Los Angeles), I relied on others for transport. Chris and a couple of his friends picked me up every morning and we drove to work together. Although Chris had believed in Jesus since his early teens, being a musician, he listened to a wide range of music, including rock and roll which, despite any reservations I had once harbored about the temptations of the "world," had long been one of my favorite musical genres. Plus, he was, as was I, eager and willing to examine how we could apply the teachings of Christianity to achieve social justice. He yearned to learn how to leverage his faith to tend to the marginalized and disadvantaged among us. We clicked almost immediately.

When Chris was sixteen, roughly ten years before I met him, he dove into a swimming pool and, because he had misjudged the depth of the water, hit the bottom. Instantly, he became a quadriplegic. He would never walk again.

Chris had been an artist since he was very young and, like most artists, had a very active imagination. He also had a wry sense of humor. Happily, despite his severe injuries, he was able, with the assistance of some cleverly designed prosthetics, to draw and write. In addition to graphics work for the organization for whom we were both employed, he did freelance work. In fact, a number of years after I left Dallas at the end of the summer to return to seminary in California, Chris, too, left the organization to go out on his own. He did very well.

While I do not spend much time on Facebook, I occasionally scan the news feed in hopes of finding notable updates in the lives of my Facebook "friends." One day about seven years ago, I came upon one of Chris's posts. "Today is the 45th anniversary of my accident," he wrote, "I'm so thankful it happened."

Wow. Here he is, unable to walk, unable to dress or clean himself, consigned to a wheelchair until the day he dies, and he is thankful. I was amazed.

Would I, however, really expect anything else? Chris's faith is not in what God does or does not do in this life. His faith is who God is. Not necessarily *in* who God is, but simply *that* God is. Chris believes that because God *is*, God redeems. He believes that, regardless of the hopelessness of a situation, because God is, it is not beyond God's ability to redeem it. It is not beyond God's ability to realize a greater purpose, a greater purpose that rises, phoenix like, from the ashes of this worldly tragedy.

If I am to believe in the fact of this purpose, however, I must live in tomorrow, today. I must believe in a fullness that is here, yet a fullness which has yet to clearly appear. I must understand that I will not see *full* redemption, spirit, body, and soul, in this existence. On the other hand, however, I must accept that, in a highly enigmatic way, I will: my faith is understanding, and trusting, that the future has already come.

Such paradox isn't always easy. In a world in which natural and supernatural flow seamlessly together and I have only my fractured epistemology to differentiate between them, I often have difficulty in discerning divine purpose amidst the good and bad that characterize human existence. It's absolutely there, yes, but it's not.

In referring to those who believed in God prior to the advent of Jesus, the writer of the letter to the Hebrews notes that, "They died in faith, without receiving the promises . . . [but] make it clear that they are seeking a country of their own" (Hebrews 11:13-14). These early believers lived their entire life without seeing the fulfillment of their faith's promise. They had to accept that it was enough to know that God, and his promise, were there.

It was a fearsome fate. So it is for me. In affirming the supernatural shape of reality, I also acknowledge the tension, the elemental and enormously powerful tension pervading this reality. I'm reminded that, as I have noted earlier, I walk through a deeply jumbled world, a world in which chaos and order collide constantly, a world of deafening shadow and achingly silent light. It is a world in which I will rarely know how purpose comes together. It is a world in which all I know is that God is there, actively working and cultivating meaning in the farthest reaches of the cosmos.

And this has to be enough.

But sometimes we'd like to see more. Since I was seven

years old, I've stuttered. At times I've stuttered quite severely; at other times, barely at all. Either way, over sixty years later, my stuttering is still with me. And I with it. There have been times in my life when I have felt rather hopeless about my stuttering, times when I despaired of ever speaking more fluently. Conversely, there have been times when I have been relatively content with it, reasonably prepared to accept it as my lot.

So, I'm told, per the message of Christian faith, that although I may live with a degree of unhappiness regarding my stuttering in this life, one day I will stutter no more. One day, I will be transformed into a beingness unlike anything that, in this life, I can imagine. One day, all things being equal, I will be the fullest expression of myself, an expression unaccompanied by any and all earthly impediments, be they physical, mental, or emotional. I will be like Jesus, living a "celestial" existence free of all earthly flaw and shortcoming.

On the other hand, as Chris's condition is for him, so my stuttering is for me: both are part of who we are. Who would we be without them? You can't imagine, many Christians nonetheless tell me, you just can't imagine what mobility or not stuttering will be like. You can only believe it will one day be true. Fair enough. But it's still difficult, in this present moment, to picture.

Consider one of my seminary roommates named Dave. Over forty years ago, high on the slopes of Alaska's Mt. Denali, Dave was forced to spend a night without sleeping bag or shelter. He ended up losing all his fingers and toes. Yet Dave is who he is today in large part because of his accident. Were his appendages to be restored, he'd be an entirely different person. Were he, in heaven, to find himself fully restored physically, who would he then be?

Herein is the crux. Yes, faith understands that present weakness (and weakness is a dicey term) is part and parcel of present existence. An infinite love does not wend its way through finitude without pain. Yet faith also understands that, in God's universe, weakness is, ironically enough, the pathway to its own annihilation. It is an annihilation, however, whose full picture, in this life, faith will likely never see. All faith knows is that in a world in which the fact and presence of God is the central and integrating thread, our weaknesses are, as Chris poignantly implied, the final meeting place of human desire and divine love in a broken universe. That in this indecipherable entanglement of breakdown and redemption all things will find hope and home. Or as Mary, Queen of Scots, wrote into a tapestry she embroidered while awaiting execution in sixteenth century England, "Virtue flourishes with a wounding."

Resurrection is amazing, and resurrection is perplexing: I will never know, stuttering and all, how it will be. I must trust that the presence of God is as much foundation as it is end.

Toward the end of his second letter to the church at Corinth, Paul recounts a journey in which he was "caught" up into "Paradise" and heard "inexpressible words, which a man is not permitted to speak." After experiencing this, Paul adds, he could easily have boasted: after all, he saw a vision of heaven. But, he notes, God, so as to keep him from "exalting" himself, gave him a "thorn in the flesh." Paul does not tell us what this "thorn" was, only that it made life and ministry considerably more difficult for him.

Paul prayed many times to God for relief. Eventually, God told him that, "My grace is sufficient for you, for power is perfected in weakness." Paul didn't need answers, Paul didn't need resolution. He only needed God's grace.

God would take care of everything else.

Accepting grace's sufficiency, however, does not come without pain. My journey with Jesus has been far from easy. It has taken me into some of the most difficult periods of my life. My capacity and willingness to believe has been pushed to its limits over and over again. And beyond. I have had to learn repeatedly, that although God's grace is sufficient in all things, I will only find this sufficiency through weakness, hardship, and failure. Having said this, let me also say that I would never presume that, from a worldly standpoint, my struggles, hardships, and failures have been greater than those of others. Far from it. I do believe, however, that it is my faith, and not the struggles, hardships, and failures themselves, that have made them so difficult. I'm always wondering about the fact of God.

Sufficiency can be hard. But it's good. For instance, nearly every person who has sat under my teaching comments on the depth of my wisdom. It's humbling. And gratifying. But as a student I've known nearly twenty-five years once pointed out to me, it's wisdom hard won. Indeed. Any wisdom I may possess is the fruit of years and years of wrestling what I see with the sufficiency of what I do not. It is the effect of learning, repeatedly upon repeatedly, to appreciate the struggles, weaknesses, and failures of the moment through the lens of the greater sufficiency, the greater purpose, a purpose here, a purpose to come.

A sufficiency and purpose in a moment which has already made itself known.

If I believe it.

In his first letter, John writes, "Beloved, we are children of God, and it has not appeared yet as to what we will be. We know that when He [Jesus] appears we will be like Him, because we will see Him just as He is." (1 John 3:2)

John captures my angst perfectly. I am loved by God, yes, but I cannot now see this love's final expression. All I know, and must believe, is that, in the final hour, to use a bit of eschatological terminology, I will. I will see Jesus make himself definitively known to me: I will see him as he is. I will see, visibly, the love of God.

Whatever this will look like. And whatever my "weaknesses" will then be.

Many years ago, I read C. S. Lewis's *Chronicles of Narnia.* Its six volumes tell a tale of a land, a mystically delightful land of witches, dragons, mountains, forests, talking animals, and Aslan, the wise and mighty lion who oversees it all. Narnia, however, is a land into which not everyone can go. Narnia only opens itself to those who believe in it. And, significantly, those who will come to believe in it. Narnia is a land in which people come to know who they most are. Yet Narnia's revelations do not come easily. They are promises which the humans who enter Narnia must often wait many years to see.

A life unburdened of sin and darkness is a life of untold wonder. Absolutely. The road to it, a road of hardship, failure, and weakness, however, is not. Faith's paradox is that living unbound by time or space is not possible without first knowing the wreckage of finitude's fallenness. Memory's transcendence is born in the shoals of temporal experience.

Even if one day we will be like God.

Barely a month after my conversion experience in Jasper, I traveled, via Greyhound Bus, from Regina, Saskatchewan, to Vancouver, British Columbia. We took Highway 2, the lonely highway that threads through the hinterlands of southern Canada, stopping at every conceivable habitation along the way. With much time on my hands to think, pray, and ponder, I decided to read two venerable volumes of classical Christian thought, Hannah Hurnard's *Hind's Feet on High Places* and *Mountains of Spices*, given to me by a "little old lady" I met in a Christian bookstore outside Regina. These books told me of the story of a spiritual pilgrim, a person who longed to see God. She wanted to see the bigger part of the reality that she believed was there. You will see me, God told her, but you must endure a great deal of pain and unhappiness to do so. For, God added, it is only through this turmoil that you will become like me. Insight and glory will not come without travail and pain.

This woman therefore had to cross many rivers and scale many mountains to find her place, to find the fullness of who she could be in her belief in God. It was a frightfully arduous journey. Tucked comfortably into my bus seat, I frequently found myself weeping over her pain, trembling at what God was asking this woman to experience. What awaits me?

As it turned out, God was trying to get this pilgrim to understand that she had to experience the sufferings of a suffering God in order to find who this God, this God of love, most is. He would not appear before she did.

Even if she was a child of God.

Faith's an arduous hope. It's also terrifying. Consider Job's conclusion about wisdom. After surveying the work of humanity in digging for iron, gold, and precious stones and its efforts to use the mountains and rocks of the world for its welfare, Job asks (28:12), "But where can wisdom be found? And where is the place of understanding?" Its value cannot be measured in earthly terms, he adds, and its origins are obscure. Where can it be?

At the end of the chapter, Job concludes that, "It is the fear [reverence] of the Lord that is wisdom." Wisdom is not something to be "found" like iron or a rare earth mineral. It is rather something that comes out of a willingness to trust God above all else. It grows out of the way we trust God to see and deal with the world. My faith is not something I find, nor is it something I earn. It's not even something I exercise, although I do "have" faith in Jesus. My faith is an experience, an experience I cannot create, yet an experience which does not happen without me wanting it to. It's not a state of mind, nor is it a condition of spirit and soul. But it cannot happen without all of these coming together. Faith is who I am, yet it is also bigger than who I am. I cannot pin it down. Nor can I label it and put it into a box on my bookshelf. My faith is an experience that undergirds and shapes all my other experiences, yet it is not an experience that I can touch apart from them. It's unique, but not alone. Faith is at once how I live, why I live, and what I live for. It's a passion and dedication, journey and goal, commitment and desire. It is everything that there is for me. In a way, my faith and I are one.

My faith therefore grows in me without me really

thinking about it, like a flower whose seed seems to sprout "magically" from the soil; or a river that, slowly and imperceptibly, swallows ever greater stretches of shore as it proceeds to the sea. I can't "see" the flower or river "grow." I only see their growth's effects. Similarly, I don't try to "make" faith; I live it. And it lives in me. Sure, in prayer and bible study I might be able to deepen my understanding of my faith, but these in themselves do not source or "increase" my faith. Faith isn't about seeking proof of itself; it's about living life with God.

Also, as I have hinted frequently to this point, my faith is about relationship. It is about walking in a relationship of trust with God. Though my faith begins with belief, a reasoned and intelligent assent to the presence and love of God, I experience it most fully in direct and continuous communion with this God. And as we shall often see as we tread further into this narrative, it is in this idea of relationship that everything about faith ultimately comes together.

Hence, if I am asked, as I often am, in my atheist discussion group what it would take for me to abandon my faith, I reply that it is not a matter of simply no longer believing in God. While I acknowledge to the questioner that rejecting my faith would pose significant epistemological challenges, I add that these do not constitute faith's heart. It is relationship.

But curiosity lingers. Throughout the Bible, the reader is admonished and encouraged to, as an old hymn goes, "Carry everything to God in prayer." God, the believer is told, hears and answers prayer. Moreover, some passages say, not only will God hear and answer the believer's prayer; he will answer it in the way that she wishes for him to.

This is quite a promise. Yet it also seems to make faith, and God, instruments of utility, little more than mechanisms for redressing the sundry challenges of life. It seems to view God as a giant slot machine.

Maybe. To repeat, however, faith is not transactional. It is a relationship. I've been running for over thirty years. When I say running, I mean that for over thirty years I've intentionally made time to run and, moreover, have made gradual improvement in my times. Initially, I ran around the park across the street from our apartment. In the midst of some very challenging graduate studies, spending hours and hours with my head buried in books, I felt as if I needed to get outside, to get some fresh air, and stretch my body. To give my body—and mind—a break. Because I hadn't ran systematically before, I ran every day. Big mistake. After a couple of weeks, I realized my right knee hurt. The more I ran, the more I hurt. When I finally saw an orthopedic surgeon, he told me I had a very common injury called runner's knee. It wasn't a big deal, he said, just stop running for a while. He gave me a referral for some physical therapy.

After a few weeks of rest and therapy, I returned to running. This time, however, I was more careful. I didn't run every day. The following summer, however, I read an article about a sport called triathlon. A sport in which I could combine swimming, bicycling, and running. A sport in which I wouldn't be competing with anyone except myself. A sport that would offer me opportunity to train in a range of activities, to exercise my entire body in the course of a week. I got a book and started training. By the beginning of the next winter, I was swimming thousands of yards a week, running five to seven miles at a time, and bicycling twenty or twenty-five miles with ease. When snow started falling, I put my bike up on a stand and continued to put on the miles. Come spring, I got out again and was soon riding forty and fifty miles with very little effort, running ten and twelve miles without thinking about it, and swimming and swimming and swimming, going through multiple swimsuits and sets of goggles. I was fitter than I had ever been in my life.

Although after thirty-five years into it I no longer train to actively compete (except to do a half Ironman to celebrate my sixtieth birthday), I continue to work out in all three sports. One day, a day only three years ago, however, I got news I had long dreaded. I had developed a stress fracture. In all my years of running, I had only incurred minor injury. I was never down long. Now, perhaps it had caught up with me. So I had to stop running, completely, for two to three months.

Waiting turned out to be easier than I thought. I got more sleep, spent more time with Carol, took things easier. Nonetheless, I counted the days until I could return to running.

One morning, however, changed all of this. As I was coming down my stairs one day, one of my crutches (I had been on crutches to take the weight off my injured leg) slipped and I came down full force on my injured leg. Ouch. I had fractured the neck of my femur. Immediate surgery was required. The surgeons put three pins in me, and I seemed as good as new.[5]

An x-ray I had twelve weeks later was not as sanguine. For a number of reasons, not all of which the doctors could figure, my fractured bone was not healing. We could still see the fracture line in the bone.

A hip specialist had the solution: a new hip. It's not a solution any runner wants to hear. People with hip replacements cannot run (unless they wish to endure another surgery, euphemistically called "a revision," in ten years). My running "career," such as it was, would be over.

So I prayed. I didn't pray that my hip would "magically" heal and I wouldn't need surgery. That's not what relationship is all about. Being in a relationship of faith is not to demand that everything goes the way I want. It is to understand that everything that goes, goes within a framework of eternal purpose. Nothing is random, nothing is unredeemable: everything has purpose and point. In faith's relationship, I bridge the dividing line, the mysterious and fragile dividing line between the certainty of physical breakdown and the unassailable fact of an eternal God. I do not confront bentness that is beyond straightening to necessarily straighten it, but rather to trust that such things are being woven into a divine drama of far larger proportion.

---

[5] The other part of the story is that I "slipped" right before Carol and I were to catch a taxi to O'Hare airport and fly to see Spruce (his real name is Bruce), one of my dearest friends, and his wife Karen in Boise, Idaho. Not knowing the extent of my injury, I opted to get on the airplane anyway. I got the news of the fracture the next day after Karen, a retired nurse, encouraged me to go to the emergency room. Carol and I laugh that I had to fly all the way to Boise to get my femur repaired!

Consider Jesus. At the moment of his greatest agony on the cross, he cried out, "My God, my God, why have you forsaken me?" Did Jesus no longer hope or believe? Not a chance. Jesus' faith was far more than intellectual assent. It was about relationship. As the Son of God, God in human flesh, Jesus had an unbreakable relationship with God. His acceptance of his fate, his God given destiny, was the fruit of his heart communion with God.

Jesus knew that faith's greatest point was its eternal purpose.

But he still cried out. As do we. Not without reason did the writer of Psalm 116 observe, "I believed when I said, 'I am greatly afflicted'." Had Jesus not believed, he wouldn't have cried out to God. So it is with me. I cry out to God precisely *because* I believe, because I have hope. I cry out because I have faith: I trust in the fact of God and his presence.

But trust can be fearsome. The day after Mom died, I rose early, grabbed one of the cars in the driveway, and drove to the beach. It was about 7:00 a.m. I saw no one else on the sand. Good: I was happy to be alone. I watched the waves, the waves on which Bob and I had spent so many happy afternoons, surfing and riding the blue, Mom always watching us from her chair on the top of the tidal berm. I remembered how, as we grew older, she let us go to the beach alone. We lingered in the water for hours, Bob and I, our eyes constantly scanning the waves rolling in from the west, our hearts always ready for another ride. I also thought about how one summer, our minds filled with images of the many huge redwood trees we had seen during a recent family camping trip to Sequoia National Park, we took to naming the waves which, come around four o'clock, were rising six, eight, and ten feet high, after the trees we had seen.

On this morning, this morning after I watched my mother die, I scanned the skies again. Even though the month was July, they were still cloudy and gray: a typical Los Angeles summer beach "gloom." With a smile, I recalled the countless hours I had spent under this ashen canopy, reading every piece of radical political literature I could find: Marx, Proudhon, Goldman, Trotsky, Mao, Lenin, Marcuse, and many, many more. Then I looked at the Santa Monica Mountains rising to the north. After forty years, they hadn't changed a bit: still glorious, enticing, and green.

I also remembered how, three days after Dad had died some twenty-seven years before, Mom took us four kids to the same beach. Once we got to the water, she left us to our own conversations and started walking up the beach, alone. No one asked to accompany her. We knew she needed her space. As did we. As I watched her, I looked across the ocean. This time, the sun was shining and the waves sparkled in the October sun. Santa Catalina Island lay to the west, its bisected landmass hovering on the sea and, to the south, the Palos Verdes Peninsula, the Peninsula on which I had done so many zany and crazy things in high school, thrust into the salty blueness.

Then I remembered that night, that October night many, many moons ago, when Mom called me to say that Dad had unexpectedly died. I cried all night: Dad was gone, irretrievably lost and gone. I'd never see him again, never, never. Even if I lived a hundred and fifty years, I would never see my father again. It was over.

That night, I reminded myself, was probably the darkest of my life. Never had I felt so totally hollow, so utterly helpless. Death had come, and I had no good answer for it. Nothing I could say made sense. Yes, I tried to believe, and yes, I tried to pray. I tried to believe that God was good. I tried to tell myself that God cared, that God was concerned, that purpose remained. That God was there.

That was really all I could say.

I also reminded myself that I chose to trust God that night not because he would undo Dad's death, though I knew full well he could, but rather precisely because he probably *would not.* I trusted and prayed because I believe in freedom, mine and that of the universe. I believe in me, I believe in God. I believe in the reality of a broken world, I believe in the truth of God. To recall Isaiah 55, which I shared earlier, God's ways are not mine. Nor do I want them to be. I want God to behave differently than I; I want God to work in ways other than those I might employ. I want a bigger picture. Even if I do not understand it fully.

"For what should I now hope?" I said to God that foggy July morning, "to what should I now direct my prayers?" I felt overwhelmed, overwhelmed by, in fact, God. I at once loved and feared him. I affirmed purpose, yet I felt absence. Though I was finding solace and meaning, I was also finding mystery and opacity. I knew, however, that I could not believe without both. If terror means to arouse fear by causing uncertainty or pain, well, then that is exactly what God promises to those who seek to believe and hope in him. They will live in great joy, they will live with biting bewilderment. But they will also live knowing that nothing is without point.

Even after death and all things earthly are said and done.

Faith is as wondrously alluring as it is maddeningly exasperating.

Nearly ten years ago, after backpacking together for a few days in the Bishop Creek region of the Eastern Sierra Nevada, Payson and I split up so that each of us could backpack a few days alone. Although I had solo backpacked countless times, Payson had not. And he very much wanted to do so. It was time: he was almost twenty years old. On our third morning in, we broke camp, hiked to the crest of 11,000 foot Muir Pass (named after the famous Scottish born naturalist who founded the Sierra Club) and, after taking in the vistas together, bade each other farewell.

It was bittersweet.

Sunny skies reigned our first two days apart. Crisp mornings, deeply blue and green meadows and lakes, magnificently starry nights. Late in the night of the second day, however, a storm swept across the range. Camped in a lake basin below a 12,000 foot pass, snug in my tent, I listened to the sky shake with thunder, cracking, crashing, and pouring down not sprinkles, but literal inches of rain. Although I felt secure enough in my tent, I worried how long the deluge would last. Few tents are designed for a monsoon. And I worried about Payson, many miles away, alone, braving the storm on his own. I could do nothing for him.

By early morning, the rain had stopped. Rising before sunrise, I ate a quick breakfast, broke camp, and headed east, over the pass, hoping to get to lower elevations, where I would have more shelter in which to camp. I arrived at my camp well before dinner, and spent the afternoon reading David Mitchell's *Cloud Atlas,* a hoary and complex tale of disconnected yet mutually empty lives and times, and sipping tea, nary a cloud in sight.

As I got into my sleeping bag that night, I heard rain falling. Pitter, patter, pitter patter. No concerns. My sleeping bag was warm, my stomach was full, and I had a good tent. Around midnight, however, I thought differently. Lightning and thunder were rocking the skies, ripping the night's once burbling ambience apart. I peeked out of my tent to see the peaks under which I was camped as bright as day, their summits lit, as if on fire, by near constant fulgurations of the angry storm. I was in awe. I was looking at the mountains' dark side, their hidden underbelly, the long gone atavistic meteorological and geological upheavals that birthed them.

Then things took a bad turn: water began to enter my tent. As I write these words today, I say that, as I stated above, few tents are designed to withstand a monsoon. The volume of water coming down that night was so much that it overwhelmed all the defenses my little tent could mount. Also, although I had chosen my tent site carefully, I had not anticipated that a gully would form in the ridge on which I was camped, a gully that pushed its way down from a mountainside over a mile away: who would have thought? As a result, my tent was sitting on what was becoming a near torrent of water. Despite my sleeping pad, forming as it did a barrier between me and the tent floor, I would soon be soaked.

What to do? Naturally, the first thing I did was pray. With words that, in retrospect, seem rather arrogant, even puerile, I asked God to stop the rain, to halt these torrents of water that were threatening me with inundation. I asked him to bring an end to the storm, to do whatever he needed to do to end this madness.

Then I stopped. Was this storm really random? Was it really just a happenstance, a natural result of the weather patterns in high mountains? Had God known about this storm in advance? From all eternity, had he been aware that it would come? If so, and if he is present and working in my life, why did he land me at this lonely and isolated lake? Couldn't he have led me somewhere else?

On the other hand, the whole thing seemed rather inane. Who was I, really, asking God to look down on me, nervous and battered but well fed and healthy me, one person out of seven and a half billion, a person who is in these mountains not by force, circumstance, or compulsion? I was not a forgotten shepherd leading his meager flock over the barren slopes of Afghanistan, wanting only to earn a little money for his family. Nor was I a Yakut in northern Siberia who, in sub-zero weather, was setting traps for sables, hoping to sell their extraordinarily supple fur to people who will make high priced coats for wealthy Russians. I'm just another affluent Westerner seeking adventure and solace in mountains, mountains in which I grew up, yes, but mountains out of which I would soon return to a life of four walls, electricity, and indoor plumbing, a life of comfort and privilege. I didn't *have* to be here.

Foolish man!

It was one thing to ask God to heal one's daughter or provide consolation in the aftermath of a parent's passing. Deliverance from a mountain storm? My life was not in danger. Other than getting really wet, I would be all right.

I was only four miles from the trailhead; I could easily hike out the next morning. What's the big deal?

I thought back several decades to my graduate studies at the University of Chicago. For a few months of that time, I participated in a sporadically scheduled discussion group led by the dean of Rockefeller Chapel. One day, he sent us a short note with this question: does God act?

Even then, I knew very well that I was not an independent agent, an autonomous soul detached from everything else around me. I lived with an infinite God in a universe too vast for me to comprehend, a God who presides over a massive and ever expanding coalescence of plasma and cosmic dust beyond imagination. I was fooling myself if I thought I knew how God acts.

Moreover, at that point, I was barely a decade—a very full decade—removed from my "dark night of the soul" in the mountains of Jasper. It had been a decade of great joy and wonder yet also one of much confusion, sorrow, and pain. Indeed, as I thought about the dean's question that day, I could not help but remember how, just eight years before, while I was attending seminary, I woke up one morning to realize that I didn't even have two dollars to my name.

I also thought about Dad. As the years continued to roll by after his death, it seemed as if his passing was only the beginning. Barely a month had elapsed when Lynn, a dear college friend, called me to say that Jackie, one of our most beloved comrades, always adventurous, always strong, had tried to take her own life. Why, I thought, would Jackie do such a thing? How had life turned her to take such a drastic step of release?

I wondered whether God really loved her.

About a year after this, to enlarge on a recollection I shared earlier, I received a call from Mom telling me that my favorite uncle, Uncle Art, had died. Art was even younger than Dad: he had yet to celebrate his sixtieth birthday. What next?

It didn't take long to find out. The following spring, I got yet another call from Mom: my last surviving grandfather (her father) had died. Throughout my life, Grandpa had been such a loyal person, a welcome and welcoming friend. Regardless of what cultural or religious turns I had made over the years, irrespective of any opinions I entertained or held, Grandpa never wavered in his love and affection for me. Because he and Grandma had lived close by when we were growing up, I saw him almost every week. When I got off the phone, I felt as if I had lost the final pillar of my childhood. What I had long known and that on which I had long relied, consciously or not, suddenly, and swiftly, was no more.

As the rain continued to seep into my tent, I recalled the discussion that the five of us had about the Dean's question. How we bantered, how we danced, how we flitted about it like medieval scholastics. Although we all agreed that God acts, we could not understand, much less say, *how* he does. All we could say is that God always acts in love.

Yet even this conclusion, a conclusion that shouted at us from almost every page of the Bible, raised questions. What about hell, we asked? What about mentally or physically challenged newborns? What about torture and war? And so on.

We knew we were not robots. Neither was God.

Furthermore, I repeated to myself that rainy mountain night, the world will always spin according to its innate rhythms, the patterns with which it is intrinsically endowed, the patterns into which it has settled since the day it came into existence. The sun shines, the rivers flow, animals hunt, and plants grow. Storms, big and small, happen, too. Thunder rumbles, lightning flashes. And rain falls, sometimes in sprinkles, sometimes in floods. It's the nature of what is. And God is not likely to undo these patterns and rhythms for little old me.

I also thought about Payson. I knew, from years of experience, that a storm of this magnitude would spread a wide net across the range. I feared for him. I feared that he was being mercilessly pummeled in his little tent. That his first solo was proving to be a near disaster. Why couldn't, I asked whimsically, God at least help him?

More darkly, I wondered why God, as far as I can tell, will watch a tornado level one house and, for some unfathomable reason, watch it avoid the one adjoining it. What kind of a God is he, anyway? I struggled to divine the interplay of God's choice and the cosmos's freedom. I struggled to reconcile moment and eternity, to connect the random instant and the everlasting vision.

I tried very hard to grasp this storm's "moment."

But I couldn't. On the one hand, I knew that, if God is indeed there, all this cannot be random. On the other hand, it can't all be planned, either. What am I therefore to do? Granted, I knew there was a reason, a solid meteorological reason, why rain and thunder and lightning are this night rocking my world. This storm didn't come out of nowhere. For all of its breakdowns, the world remains a finely tuned machine, a well oiled system of orderly and largely intelligible processes.

Furthermore, as I stretched out in my sleeping bag for the umpteenth time, I told myself that, all science aside, I, like Job of centuries ago, will drive myself batty if I try to look for metaphysical reasons. In fact, I wasn't convinced that this was even a legitimate question. There are no whys to God; there is only God.

It's about meaning, I concluded, it's about meaning. I therefore should not even try and figure out why, in the compass of the divine vision that is constantly rippling through human existence, I am here, this night, in this storm. That's not the issue. I'm here. And nowhere else.

Nonetheless, I wondered, again, whether this carefully constructed schemata of orthodox Christianity I had come to inhabit, this schema, built as it is around a God who is spirit yet who is also extraordinarily personal and supremely cognitive, can possibly be true. Once again, I questioned why this God, this perplexing God to whom I had devoted my life for at that point nearly forty years, had to be. And act.

It's a brutal world. And an even more brutal faith.

Sure, I knew all the arguments for the necessity and existence of God. Yes, I knew that, as John's gospel explains, in Jesus we see God. And I knew, knew absolutely, that had I not invited Jesus into my life over forty years before this night, I would still be looking for permanence of meaning and purpose. Absolutely no argument there.

Yet I was also very much aware that these truths are simply inklings of a far larger one. As I noted earlier, God is not a point, nor does he have a point. God *is* point. The fact of God is *the* meaning of the universe. There is nowhere in the cosmos devoid of God's beingness, no place where he is not. My wondering about whether God acts or loves, though it often makes me writhe with discomfort and befuddlement, is therefore, no pun intended, beside the point. My far greater task is to believe that, all these misgivings notwithstanding, God is the beginning, end, and everything in between. To return to Acts 17, which I mentioned earlier, it is in this God that, "We live and breathe and have our being."

On the other hand, insisting that God is everywhere often leads me to conclude that he is nowhere. I'm still fighting to hold on to the point.

The wonder is remarkable, the pain is exquisite.

A strong and adventurous young man, Zane was one of my nephews on Carol's side of the family. Over twenty-five years ago Carol and I received word that Zane, who at the time was stationed with the U.S. Navy in Oman, had perished in a flash flood in the mountainous deserts outside Muscat.

As the family grieved, the last thing we needed to hear, or think, was there was a reason, a plan. That in his infinite wisdom God wanted Zane to die. What did this make God to be?

Simple: the ultimate ogre and puppeteer.

Again, I said that mountain night, purpose isn't about why. It's about sufficiency, the sufficiency of grace. It's about viewing faith, and trust, in the present love of God as enough to keep going, even in the face of unresolvable questions.

Otherwise, I reminded myself, thinking about the horrific tsunami that, without warning, had risen out of the Pacific Ocean off Indonesia on December 26, 2004, and killed, in the space of a few minutes, over 250,000 people, I would need to say that, oh, there's a reason for this. Or when militaries or police officers across the world kill innocent people, people who were guiltless of whatever it was that these officials insisted they did, or people who, for no fault of their own, are caught in a misdirected aerial bombing of their home and subsequently die, I would need to say that God had a plan, a reason, an intelligible and sensible reason why he allowed this to happen. Or if a woman is viciously raped, well, God has a plan.

The thought makes me shiver.

This is what makes faith so terribly, terribly difficult. In saying that it is not about why, in asserting that it is not about reason, in insisting that it need not know it all, faith leaves me on the edge of incredulity. But faith cannot be any other way. By its very nature, my faith eviscerates everything I presently know. And it eviscerates it with everything I do not know, at least in full. My faith demands nothing less than total loyalty to the necessary truth of the unanswered question.

It's a bitter impasse.

The thirteenth chapter of the gospel of Matthew is often called the "kingdom of God" chapter. In it, Matthew, once a Jewish tax collector despised by his people but who later decided to devote his life to following Jesus and proclaiming him as Messiah, presents his assembling of Jesus' parables about the kingdom of God.

By way of explanation, I note that in Matthew 13 these parables are described as parables about the kingdom of heaven. This is due to Matthew's desire, when he put his gospel together, to compose an account relevant to his

Jewish brethren. Given that during this time most Jews were reluctant, out of respect for their maker, even to say the word "God" (indeed, to this day, many Orthodox Jews write the word God as "G-d"), Matthew chose to substitute the word "heaven" for "God" in his recounting of Jesus' life.

I mention a couple of parables in particular. The first is known as the parable of the mustard seed (this parable also appears in the gospels of Mark and Luke, the other two of what scholars call the three synoptic (from the Greek words for "same seeing") gospels). A farmer plants a mustard seed which, for Jesus' audience, was the smallest known seed, in a field, then leaves it to grow. When some time later the farmer returns to check on his work, he sees that this tiny mustard seed has grown into an enormous tree, one that is larger than all the others, one in which "the birds of the air come and nest in its branches" (a phrase which Jesus borrowed from one of the stories in the writings of the prophet Daniel). Well aware that that he did nothing to nurture it, the farmer has difficulty understanding how this tiny seed developed into such a big tree. Its outsized growth is a mystery.

The other parable is that of the leaven. A woman takes some leaven and, as we do with yeast today, worked it into some flour, then left it to do its thing. Subsequently, without the woman doing anything else, the leaven, in the peculiar way that leaven does, "grows" the flour into a piece of dough big enough to make, when baked, a loaf of bread. The woman has done nothing to help the flour along. And she does not see *how* the leaven raised the flour. The dough's growth is a mystery.

What's the point? The kingdom of God (or, in John's gospel (John 3:3)), the experience of God grows in ways that we cannot always understand. And it grows without us being conscious of how it is doing so. It grows, Jesus is saying, in a mystery. We may see its results, but we do not necessarily see how it moves toward or produces them. Faith's challenge is to therefore believe that although things will indeed, in a manner of speaking, "work out," they will do so not "just because they did" (or as some members of my atheist discussion group might say, "I guess the universe was looking out for me") but because a larger cognitive and loving presence is purposefully working in existence to ensure a greater end.

Even if we cannot see it doing so. Even if it's in mystery.

Morning finally came. I was so happy. The rain had stopped, the sky was clearing: all seemed well. Four miles lay between me and the parking lot. Four downhill miles. I packed my very moist sleeping bag into its stuff sack, folded up my rather soggy tent, stuffed an energy bar in my mouth, shouldered my pack, and took off. I didn't want to fiddle with cooking, I didn't want to take a last photo. I only wanted to get out.

An hour later, I was at our car. Another thirty minutes and I was at the parking lot where Payson said he would come out. After I had been waiting an hour, he came striding into the parking lot, looking strong, fit, and none the worse for wear. Never had I been so happy to see him. All was well.

As we talked about our respective nights, however, it became apparent that, as I had feared, the rain had hit Payson's camp hard, too. "It poured," he said. "My tent flooded. I had to move it twice."

I was too happy to see him to ask what he now thought about God.

After we checked into a hotel in Bishop, shaved, showered, and got a "real meal," we returned to our room to rest. As I lay on my bed, I thought about where I had been less than twelve hours before. What a contrast, what a change. I believed that God had been working in that long and harrowing night. I believed that he had always been there.

But I still wondered what God meant now. To paraphrase the eighteenth century German writer Novalis, if all art has, as he noted, "an *a priori* ideal," a "necessity in and of itself for being in the world," in the same way God, somehow and some way has likewise ensured that, in his compass and vision, all things have purpose, necessity, and point.

I guess. When I graduated from seminary in 1980, while I was still not precisely sure what I wanted to do vocationally, I did know that I wanted to teach. At the time, Carol and I were living in Dallas, engaged. We married a year later. Being married was wonderful; living as a West Coast seminary graduate in Dallas was not. Then, and now, the only seminary in town was Dallas Theological Seminary (DTS). With an impressive historical pedigree and a full orbed commitment to the theological perspective of dispensationalism, DTS set the standard for all bible teaching in the city.

It was a very rigid standard, too.

The seminary from which I graduated, Fuller Seminary, was a far more openminded institution of theological learning. It encouraged exploration and questioning; it invited and welcomed a variety of viewpoints into its discussion and deliberations. It was far more willing to speculate beyond fixed boundary. I thrived.

But now I was in Dallas. And I wanted to teach. I soon realized that what I considered open mindedness was, to the elders of the church we were attending, a harbinger of theological liberalism. This they could not tolerate. I therefore had to engage in some substantial persuasion to convince these elders that I was indeed qualified to teach and that I would not take those in my bible study into the throes of the doctrinal erosion that they believed was destabilizing the Christian church in America.

What did I teach? One of my favorite books of the Bible: Ecclesiastes. Ecclesiastes is one of the most enigmatic books of the scriptures. It talks of life's terminality and futility; the uselessness of laboring for money and goods that, when its owner dies, she will never see again; the futility of doing the right thing only to die at a young age while those who engage in evil deeds live very long lives; and the seemingly endlessness—and apparent pointlessness—of the rhythms of life and the cosmos: nothing ever starts and nothing ever ends.

Yet Ecclesiastes also speaks of the essentiality, presence, and point of God. Life may be futile, life may end, but God is there, always. If we therefore frame our lives in the person of God, the writer concludes, our years will have meaning beyond themselves. In this, Ecclesiastes strikes a profoundly insightful balance between the irrefutable fact of an eternal God and the unavoidable finitude and finality of human existence. I find myself going to Ecclesiastes repeatedly.

In our bible study, which Carol and I hosted weekly, we spent a good deal of time on verse 3:11. It reads, "God has made everything appropriate [beautiful or apt] in its time. He has also set eternity into the heart of man [humankind] yet so that man [humankind] will not find out the work which God has been done from the beginning even to the end."

What does it mean, we asked each other, to say that God has "made" everything appropriate or beautiful in its time? How active is he in the world? Is everything really preordained by God?

The perennial questions of faith!

One night, one person in the study suggested that verse 3:11 was telling us that we are caught in a paradox. She said that although we are bent to explore what is greater than us, to look for a bigger picture, we are also encumbered by our finitude. We will never learn everything we wish to know, nor will we ever be able to look beyond the days of our lives. Moreover, although we are made to seek the infinite and eternal, we will never see them. In this life, we will never know the full measure of reality.

She was spot on. But it's frustrating. Why can I not know?

Faith, however, is, as I have noted, not about knowing. It's about trusting. Faith is about trusting in the primal factuality of God's presence—and only this presence—to resolve, one day, every question. And to believe that, for this life, this is enough.

Easy to say. I'll wrestle with my epistemological limits until the day I die. As long as I live, I will live realizing that I know that I can know, but that I also know that I cannot.

I'm only human.

On the other hand, I suspect that we all see life in this way. We all understand that although we do not know everything, we can usually know enough to get by. And we all realize that the reason we will never know everything is that we are finite. So what's the point of faith?

It's faith's ken. Faith understands that without the idea that God, a personal God, is there, knowing anything in this life simply affirms the pointlessness of an accidental universe. It merely underscores life's, per Ecclesiastes, patent absurdity. It's knowledge of the coming dust.

A couple of years ago, I had a lengthy afternoon conversation with a young man who, although he had grown up in a strongly religious household, had, after much study and examination, come to conclude that there was no God. Yet Robert also understood that if he were to eliminate God, he had nothing with which to replace him: life would still be unknowable and frustrating. After an hour or so of discussion, I could see that Robert's fundamental issue was trust. He knew he couldn't trust the emptiness, yet he was also reluctant to trust God. He had reached an epistemological impasse.

So, I told him, you have a decision to make. Whatever you decide to trust, you'll be trusting with a degree of uncertainty. Either way, you'll be trusting in the absence of complete knowledge.

"If I can't know God," he replied, "I can't trust him. God has to be personal."

Words well said. Unless God is personal, it doesn't matter whether he's there or not.

I mentioned Cinderella very early in this meditation. She and I, along with Spruce, whom I also mentioned earlier, engaged, during the days of our revolutionary fervor, in some of the nuttiest things I have done. We lived to be wild, crazy, and rebellious. And we didn't care what anyone else thought.

As I also noted, Cinderella and I have kept in touch over the ensuing years, exchanging, roughly once a year, fifteen to twenty page letters exploring and discussing theology, science, philosophy, literature, and many, many other things. I love our interactions, I revel in our dialogues. For decades, Cinderella insisted that God cannot be personal.

A couple of years ago, midway through one of her letters, however, Cinderella observed that, "God must be personal. Otherwise, he's not worth believing."

It had taken many letters from me, spread over several decades, for Cinderella to come to this conclusion. I was amazed. If only, I thought as Robert and I parted ways that day, he could come to a similar conclusion. For unless God is personal, why would anyone trust him? It would be akin to trusting a rock.

Yet a personal God decimates as much as it resurrects. It ensures that the world speaks, yes, but it still leaves us in the dark: Jesus is long gone. Its offer of a relationship of spirit and not immediate physicality therefore often falls short. We still can't see.

Over ten years before this exchange, Cinderella lost her sister Peggy to cancer. Peggy was a particularly and, I dare say, peculiarly, funny woman. She relished doing the zaniest thing she could, to inflate her expectations for mirth to well beyond what most of us might imagine, much less desire. One winter night about thirty years ago, I visited Cinderella at her parents' house in Palo Alto, California (I happened to be in the area at the time). Toward midnight, we looked up from our talking to see Peggy come in dressed like a clown, her hair flaming red. She was blowing a horn, rattling a noisemaker, and whooping with glee. Her face was painted, her hands were covered with rings.

"Who was out tonight?" Cinderella asked.

"No one. It was just me."

Peggy never cared who was watching, and she didn't mind any criticism she received. She would do what she wanted to do, all the time, every time. On the last day of her life, as Cinderella recorded it and shared with me, Peggy received a steady stream of visitors, friends, family, admirers and onlookers. She entertained them, they entertained her. She died with a smile on her face.

Now Cinderella wonders where Peggy is. Although I could not readily tell her—I hesitate to describe, definitively, the structure of another's eternal home—I could offer her that, because God is there, and because he is personal, Peggy is somewhere. She is not void, she is not a blank space. She still *is*.

It is a broad and challenging faith, this faith that believes, this faith that hopes, this faith that trusts. It spans this life, it looks into the next. And it can't see or grasp, fully, either one. That's its burden, that's its point: regardless of earthly fact or perception, faith is committing to believe in the sufficiency of the presence and goodness of God.

For several decades, a friend of mine, a friend who, in fact, attended the same seminary as did I, has run a shelter for homeless people in Seattle. Beginning with a modest storefront in a forgotten part of Seattle's bustling downtown, Rick steadily built up an operation that today serves hundreds of homeless people, offering them meals and shelter night after night, three hundred and sixty-five nights a year. Nightwatch also offers long term housing for those who find reasonably permanent employment. After years of living in the streets, these fortunate individuals now have a home, a home in which they can wake up in the morning and to which they can return at night.

In one of his monthly newsletters, Rick noted that amidst the nightly tasks of feeding, sheltering and housing, we "keep hope alive." Precisely. Nightwatch keeps hope alive. In the midst of what could be a bastion of despair, Nightwatch offers hope. Although this is not a hope that resolves all problems and concerns, it is a hope that, in the mere act of its offering, fills hearts.

It is a hope that is, to put it differently, enough. It will not end homelessness, it will not vanquish unemployment, and it will not remove all the tents from the streets. Yet it will, at least for a night, sustain.

Faith doesn't resolve all problems, faith does not end all suffering. But it is, for now, enough. Faith's efficacy rests in its existential sufficiency, an existential sufficiency that is the expression of an eternal sufficiency, an eternal sufficiency in which all things find purpose and meaning.

But not necessarily explanation.

As Ecclesiastes 3:11 observes, we are here, God is there, and never in this life shall our knowing fully meet.

When in June 2018 U.S. Supreme Court Justice Anthony Kennedy announced he was retiring, speculation about his successor immediately flared up in the media. Will same sex marriage be declared unconstitutional? Will Roe v. Wade be overturned?

For many American Christians, the latter had been their greatest dream. This must be, they declared, the answer to our prayers. God has heard us. God really does care. At the same time, however, many other American Christians were saying quite another thing. We wondered why God is allowing a person whom we consider to be a horribly ignorant, racist, and misogynist president to make such a momentous selection, a selection that will affect us for decades to come. In addition, we wondered whether these two "hot button" issues ought to be the absolute litmus test for a person appointed to the U.S. Supreme Court. Shouldn't we be equally concerned about issues such as poverty, environmental destruction, voting equality, and immigration rights?

As I noted earlier, this can be frustrating. While Christians can agree that, for instance, Jesus is God in the flesh, a person who, after dying on the cross for human sin, rose from the dead on the third day, they find themselves disagreeing, often intensely, on many other points of doctrine. Again: no surprises here. Every believer is uniquely her own. Believers inhabit all parts of the planet. They are products of vastly different backgrounds and circumstances. We err if we expect them to agree on *everything*.

An outsider might say that this invalidates faith. God cannot be genuinely true if his people cannot agree on how he works or what he thinks. Fair enough. Complicating this epistemological tension is that, on the one hand, faith says that there is indeed an answer to every question. Yet on the other hand, faith says that, in this life, we may not see it. Faith cannot therefore guarantee that, in this life, our present positions on politics, economics, or culture will be absolutely and for all time correct. It can be very equivocal.

But God is decidedly not. Nonetheless, we live in a

capricious world, a world hounded by improbability uncertainty, and darkness. We will never see completely outside the box. We're only human.

Faith's mystery is dazzling.

Before I came to faith, as I have alluded, I participated, with millions of others, in the various revolutionary movements of the Sixties. Sometimes our efforts bore fruit; sometimes they did not. Frustration was frequent. So were anger and tears. Regardless, many of us, including me, would say, "There's always hope." Despite what we see and hear, despite this latest setback, we insisted, we can still have hope.

Did I believe it this? Absolutely. I still had faith in the integrity of the American political system, still had faith in the fundamental goodness of the nation's culture and people. I trusted that the Constitution would function as it ought, that the three branches of the government would hold each other accountable, and that fairness and equity would ultimately reign. I had faith that, one day, given the seminal structures of the system, all would be well. As one of my college professors, as he prepared to assume the reins of the Wisconsin state chapter of the American Civil Liberties Union, remarked to me, "Given what we have in this country, I firmly believe that we will win."

A few years ago, Carol and I joined several of my former revolutionary colleagues and their spouses for a spectacularly wonderful reunion in the Sawtooth Mountains of southern Idaho. It was magical beyond words. Although we had seen each other at various times over the decades since graduation, fully thirty-six years had elapsed since we had all been in the same place together (this being a gathering in upstate New

York the July of 1979). Now, bunked together in a cabin in the Sawtooth Valley for three days, we hung out, talking, eating, hiking, rafting, fishing, hot tubbing, watching the stars, and much more. We talked about what we were doing, how we had found our paths, how we had carved out our life journey and, for some, how we had found ways to continue engaging, albeit in more sedate fashion, in political activity. How we were still working for the "cause." Some of us really were making a difference in peoples' lives. We had stepped into the system that we had never stopped trusting and, to an extent, "won." Our hope had come full circle. It was visible, it was present. We saw the outcome of our beliefs.

As Spruce and Karen, our reunion hosts, lived in Boise, we all traveled there to begin our time together. After a couple of nights at their house, we caravanned to the Sawtooths. Some of us had rental cars, some of us did not. The latter rode with those who did. We took Linda, a dear and sweet woman who, though she had adopted two Native American children, never married. As we talked, she observed that to her, evangelical Christians have "this dark obsession" with homosexuality. They seem to make homosexuality, she said, the direst of all sins, the epitome of all wrongdoing, the absolute nadir of all human depravity.

I had to agree. As I observed earlier, many (but far from all) evangelical Christians seem to concern themselves with two issues and two issues only: abortion and same sex marriage. To their mind, based on their reading of various chapters of the Bible, chapters such as, for abortion, Psalm 139; and for homosexuality, Deuteronomy 18, Leviticus 20, and Romans 1, such things are uniformly condemned by God.

As I listened to Linda, I realized, again, that whether it is trusting that purpose prevails, trusting that the Bible is the most complete communication of God, trusting in the "rightness" of my political position, or trusting in the fact of eternity, I do so largely in an existential darkness. My politically active colleagues trust in what they see, that is, the code of law, the political system, and their individual organizational and scholarly prowess. I trust in what I cannot, the hidden presence of an eternal God. Is my darkness greater?

In many ways, it is. When I look back on the night of that mighty Sierra storm, as I recollect my experience of seminary penury, as I reflect on the various familial losses I have endured, and much, much more, I admit that, yes, in every instance I'm arguing for the virtue of the unseen in a material world. I'm leaning on what I cannot definitively prove. I'm looking to an unseen promise to ameliorate the seen present. On the other hand, in propounding the legitimacy of what I cannot fully see, I am in fact affirming the legitimacy of what I can see. I'm saying that what I see has purpose beyond itself. It's not vain or futile, it's not fundamentally transient. It is rather a thread, a thread of inestimable value in a far greater filament of transcendent vision.

If I believe it.

Faith's barrenness is its power. In stripping life away, it births it. In jettisoning the obvious, it invites the ambiguous. In undercutting wisdom, it calls it to shine. Faith's sufficiency is to believe what all worldly effort cannot: the work of God.

Matthew 8 and Luke 7 present the story of Jesus' encounter with a Roman centurion. Approaching Jesus in Capernaum, the centurion tells him that his personal servant is very ill, paralyzed and "tormented." When Jesus offers to come to the centurion's home, he demurs, saying that, "Lord, I am not worthy for you to come under my roof, but just say the word, and my servant will be healed."

Jesus marvels, telling the crowd that, "Truly I say to you, I have not found such great faith in anyone in Israel." Jesus could see that the centurion already believed that he could heal the servant. He didn't need to see Jesus physically do it. It was enough to know that he could.

Like the centurion, I do not need to "see" God working; I simply need to believe that he is doing so. I'll never see God in this life; this much I know. And that's fine. Really. It is enough for me to believe he's there.

In the closing lines of Psalm 73, the writer says, "The nearness of God is my good." Although at times God seems distant and unresponsive; though at times I feel as if I'm praying into a void; although occasionally I might get up from reading my Bible feeling either totally unenlightened or, worse, angry at God; and while I am often saddened and shocked by the political views of some believers, I nonetheless believe that, all things considered, God's nearness remains. I know it, I believe it, I live it.

And this is enough.

After over forty-six years of studying and teaching the Bible, I know it, and the many theologies that have sprung up to explain it, very well. Yet because I am an emotional being, I, along with every other believer who has ever lived, have, at various times, resorted to using my feelings to ground my understanding and sense of God's fact and presence. I fret,

I wonder, I question. I doubt. I let my feelings, or the lack thereof, get in the way of what I know to be true.

Again: I'm only human.

God wouldn't want it any other way. Friedrich Schleiermacher was a nineteenth century German theologian who worked assiduously to convince the Romantics of the worth and necessity of Christ. Speaking into their world of sensuality and imagination, he suggested that they think of Jesus as a sort of consciousness, a consciousness they cannot suppress, a consciousness that fills their heart, a consciousness that centers their understanding of the world. With this, he suggested, view religion as a feeling, a feeling of dependence, a feeling of dependence on God. Don't let the conclusions of your mind overwhelm the impulses of your heart.

So it with me: I feel, I believe; I believe, I feel. Faith is learning how to balance the two.

This is particularly true when I set about to define the goodness of God. I mentioned earlier my involvement in triathlons. Although my first race was not a long one—three fourths mile swim; thirty mile bike; and ten kilometer (six mile) run—because it was my first one, I didn't know what to expect. But I felt ready.

The swim barely winded me, and the bike went amazingly well. I passed dozens of people. The run proved slightly more challenging. I started off strong, cruising through the first four miles, my legs feeling good. At mile five, I could feel a little weariness, but the knowledge that I was only a mile from the finish spurred me on. I finished with a flourish, smiling broadly as I coasted down the final stretch. All in all, it had been a good first triathlon.

I was thankful to God. On the other hand, I felt funny. Yes, I understood that, in every way, be it swimming, bicycling, or running, much less quotidian activities such as eating, dressing, and sleeping, I was dependent on God. I knew that, if I were to be theologically and emotionally honest, I was, to use a passage which I mentioned earlier, categorically beholden to God for my very breath and being. Without his providential activity in sustaining, directly or not, my bodily functions, I would not be able to do any of these things. I would collapse and die.

Thousands of miles away, on each and every day I trained and raced, however, children were starving to death. Furthermore, as I enjoy the fruits of Western affluence today, other believers, people who are probably more devoted to God than I, are mired in the poverty and privation that continue to afflict too much of the planet. Life may well be God's training ground; it is also a harsh master. I therefore use the words, "God is so good to me" with care. I can't assess it, I can't compare it. I can only believe it.

As I do. But I still wonder how "good" comes together. Two weeks later, I raced again. This race was much longer. A half Ironman, it consisted of a 1.2 mile swim, 56 mile bike, and 13.1 mile run. I was looking at several hours of racing. But I had been training for months; I was confident I could finish.

The morning of the race, we were informed that the water temperature of Lake Michigan (the race took place in Milwaukee) was fifty-five degrees. Because I had grown up swimming in the chilly waters of the Pacific Ocean, however, I thought little about it. Stepping into the water changed all of that: this water was cold! I got out quickly. But as I stood on the beach in the mists of the early morning, looking at the roiling waves before me, I told myself that I had not come this far to skip the race. I ran into the lake and started swimming. Happily, once I got going, I warmed up and felt strong. It was a good swim.

To a point. When I stepped onto the beach again, I immediately realized that I did not feel well. And it wasn't because I was tired from the swim; given all my training, 1.2 miles was just a warmup. When I got to the medical tent, the attendants saw my problem right away: hypothermia. Thirty-five minutes in the frigid Lake Michigan water had lowered the temperature of my body core to unacceptable levels. My face looked gray, my heart was racing, and I shivered uncontrollably. Carol, seven months pregnant with Megan, was distraught. People escorted me to a table and bundled me up.

After two hours, I was pronounced recovered and released. What was next? It was obvious. I got on my bicycle and began my 56 mile trek through the hills and dales surrounding Milwaukee. Amazingly, even after being away from the course for two hours, I still saw and passed some riders. When I completed the circuit (it was a double loop), I started running. Once again, I passed people. I felt very strong as I cruised across the finish line, desperately far behind any time I had hoped to achieve, but by no means the last person to finish. I was thrilled. So was Carol!

I think the only time I prayed in the course of those several hours was as I approached the finish line. I thanked God for giving me the energy and determination to complete the race, I thanked him for Carol's loving support, I thanked him for enabling me to do triathlons.

I thanked him for his goodness.

As I reflect on this moment today, although I suppose I should draw the conclusion that my finishing was "good," I'm still left wondering at its larger meaning. I think back to a summer about eleven years ago when, as I mentioned early in this meditation, I taught at a pastors' conference in the little town of Chitipa, Malawi. Each night, after teaching all day, I stayed at a hotel in town. Relative to a hotel in the States, it was rudimentary. It lacked working toilet facilities—we flushed our toilets with pails of water the staff brought us each morning—and its electricity was shaky. But it had mosquito netting over each bed. And a roof.

In contrast, each night, conference attendees slept outside the church that hosted the conference. It was all they could afford. They had no blankets, no shelter, no water. One morning, they were served meat for breakfast (unfailingly polite, they always waited for us to arrive before they ate). They could scarcely contain themselves: "God is good!" they shouted.

I believe he is. But it's frequently hard to reconcile such belief with seeing and feeling.

Towards the end of his first letter to the church at Thessalonica, Paul urges his readers to give thanks to God "in all things" (1 Thessalonians 5:18). Whether things are going well or poorly for us, we are to give thanks to God. Such talk has never sat well with some of my unbelieving friends. "You're foolish," they tell me, "to always be grateful."

One morning a number of years ago, Rachel, a former colleague of mine, heard her husband tell her that he had fallen in love with another woman and was leaving her and their two children for her. He was very categorical about it, too: there would be no appeal. The marriage was definitively over. Rachel was therefore left, in her late-thirties, on her own with two young girls. Her soon to be former husband did not wish to help in any way.

As time passed, Rachel found employment, a place for her and her daughters to live and, despite the enduring pain, tried to move on. After ten years had passed, she met another man, whom she eventually married. In similar fashion, after they graduated from college, her daughters found husbands as well. Rachel and her new husband, Ron, now have several grandchildren to cherish and enjoy. It's almost a fairy tale ending.

Throughout her ordeal, even in her darkest hours, Rachel signed her emails with the phrase, "God is always good, all the time." I knew that she didn't always feel this way. I knew that she struggled mightily with what had happened. Her feelings loomed large frequently. Moreover, one could argue that Rachel was sharing this phrase simply to be hopeful, to hope against hope, to hope in the face of all reason and sense. Yet this would miss that Rachel signed with this phrase because, and only because although she had powerful feelings about her pain, she had equally, if not more, conviction that God is good. She didn't proclaim her words without reason. Rachel is as rational as anyone else. She knew full well that although voicing hope is helpful in almost any situation, it is meaningless unless it's anchored to something real. Something like God.

Well, someone might say, this is just deductive reasoning at its finest. It's just assuming that at least one thing is always true. Perhaps. On the other hand, it is just being logical. It is arguing that faith's hurdle is not so much to believe and feel the good as it seems to be present, but rather when it appears to be not. It is to trust the inherent subjectivity of intellectual certainty.

I spoke earlier about the tendency of my atheist friends to believe that things will just "work out." As one of them, Craig by name, insists, "I hold to reasonable expectation." Based on his understanding of the largely orderly processes that order the world, Craig says, he has a "reasonable expectation" that, eventually, all will be well. Or at least be well in a "reasonable" way.

Either way, however, Craig and I are basing our conviction that things will "work out" on our belief that what we feel we know is true. The mutual circularity is astonishing.

But there's more to the picture. In January 2012 I led a group of students on a backpacking expedition to the summit of Hawaii's Mauna Loa volcano, a point roughly 13,500 feet above sea level. Mauna Loa is one of the most massive mountains on the planet. Its visible bulk, spreading out over 400 square miles of Hawaii's "Big Island," is but a small part of its mass. The rest is under the rolling waters of the Pacific, a conglomerate of cooled and coiled lava of almost unfathomable size. Every island in the Hawaii Islands is the result of millions and millions of years of underwater volcanic eruptions. Once upon a time, the islands did not exist. Subsequently, over the course of many eons of time, driven by immense pressures at the earth's core, fissures began to open up in the ocean floor. Bursting madly out of these fissures into the hadal waters, lava cooled quickly, piling up into giant mounds that, over time, became islands and, in some instances, mountains, massive mountains of lava. Walk almost anywhere in the state of Hawaii, and you will eventually end up walking on lava, lava that has been building up for more years than you can grasp.

Because it is a mountain of lava rising out of and towering over an island of lava, Mauna Loa is, by some measures, not only the most massive mountain on earth, but the highest, too. From its base on the ocean floor to its visible summit, it is 48,000 feet high, nearly twenty thousand feet higher than Mt. Everest.

Getting to Mauna Loa's summit is not easy. The route to the top is a long and winding twenty mile trek from the 6600 foot high trailhead (itself at the end of a winding twenty mile road). It's a full two days hike. There is no trail, really, only cairns (carefully stacked towers of rock) that, perched on the lava, direct the hiker across miles and miles and miles of shapeless and arid hills of red and black. Hiking over the black lava is easy. Called "pahoe" lava, it's smooth, like polished onyx: one practically glides over it. The red lava is not as fun. It is sharp, jagged, and unyielding. Natives call it "aa" lava. Happily, most of the route is over pahoe lava.

The "trail" is not steep; it is just long. We made the nine miles to the first camp without too much difficulty. Despite the rise in elevation—6600 to 10,000 feet—the boys were doing well, and I had high hopes for the more strenuous trek that awaited us the next day.

As it always did (I've been on Mauna Loa four times), the day dawned brightly. After steadily rising above the clouds that covered the jungles and plantations far below, the sun burst into our view, illuminating the red and black lava with a rich orange glow. The sky sparkled in hues of deep blue, and Mauna Kea, the still active volcano on the other side of the valley, gleamed, its snowy cap burning in the morning light. It seemed a perfect day to hike.

We started strong and continued so well into the afternoon. By 4:30 p.m. we were at 12,000 feet, only three miles from the summit. Then things deteriorated. One member of our party, a guy who had never been at such altitude before, began to show signs of altitude sickness, and slowed his pace considerably. He was averaging less than a mile an hour. The rest of us felt strong, but the sun was dipping behind the other side of the volcano's crater and the evening winds were coming up. We were soon immersed in darkness. But we couldn't stop where we were. There was no water (the only way to get water on the volcano was to access rain barrels at our first camp and on top) and certainly no shelter. We'd be at the mercy of the wind all night.

After we put on more clothes and donned our headlamps, we separated. Payson, whom I had brought as the other chaperone, took the three strongest guys and forged ahead to the top. I navigated between them and the ailing member of the party, encouraging him, with the help of another student, to keep going. We would all meet at the summit.

After about forty-five minutes of hiking, we—the four of us moving somewhat ahead—saw, from a distance, the light of the hut (the National Park Service maintains a shelter and various meteorological instruments on top) on the summit. We knew we were almost home.

When the four of us stepped into the hut, we immediately sat down at one of the tables and prayed. We prayed for the two guys, one who was among the strongest members of the party, the other the weakest, as the latter struggled with the altitude, trying desperately to catch a breath in the thin air. We prayed for their safety, we prayed for their strength. We prayed for their imminent arrival.

Not too long after we prayed, the other hikers appeared, tired (at least one of them) but happy. They had made it. We were all together for the night.

God is good, we all agreed. We could see it, we could feel it, we believed it.

Really? Why does God not then help a child starving to death in the Central African Republic? A person being tortured in Iran?

Hard questions. Questions for which I have no ready answer.

The abyss is petrifying.

Romans 8:29 tells us that, Romans 8:28 and its promise that God will work everything for good notwithstanding, God's deepest good for the believer is conformity to the image of Jesus. It's not a material good; it's a richer spiritual experience. Meshing this good with worldly good, however, makes for some complex choreography. I'll never know why some of us experience high measures of material or emotional comfort while others do not. I'll never know how such good, or an apparent paucity thereof, aligns with God's desire to conform us to the image of Jesus. Hence, I tread cautiously when I connect God's goodness with what appears to be answered prayer. Or with how I feel about a particular situation. There is so much, so very much I cannot see about the vision of God. As it is in regard to political positions, so it is in regard to good: I will rarely get it perfectly.

Again: I'm a creature of equivocality wrestling with an unequivocal God.

We all had questions that frigid December night on the summit of Mauna Loa. And we all had doubts. Yet we knew that we felt more comfortable in doubting and questioning certain presence than in looking for the result of "reasonable" expectation, and be done with it. While doing the latter may appear, outwardly, to be more "reasonable," it in fact does little more than avoid the issue. Though I wrestle mightily with the point and efficacy of prayer, I choose to accept its mystery over one that I can make on my own. Whether I do or do not understand is not the point. More important is that I recognize that there is a point.

And mere "reasonable" expectation does not provide it. I still live and die in my passion.

I will never know why God seems to answer some prayers in the way I would like him to and some in ways which I do not always understand. But I understand that, as Paul writes to the church at Colossae, in Jesus "all things hold together" (Colossians 1:17). Unlike William Butler Yeats's oft quoted contention (in his "Second Coming") that, "Things fall apart, the center cannot hold," I can attest, attest absolutely, that in God, the center will always hold.

Precisely how, however, I will likely never know.

The book of the prophet Daniel tells the story of three young Jewish men named Shadrach, Meshach, and Abed-nego. As the writer tells it, the Neo-Babylonian king Nebuchadnezzar one day built a ninety foot high gold image of himself and ordered, on pain of death, his subjects to worship it. Being Hebrews who were completely devoted to Yahweh, whom they considered to be the one true

God, Shadrach, Meshach, and Abed-nego refused to do so. Nebuchadnezzar was enraged. He demanded that these Hebrews be arrested and cast into a "furnace of blazing fire."

Before having them thrown into the flames, the king gave the men one more chance to repent. Their reply has become the fodder of many a sermon:

> "O Nebuchadnezzar, we do not need to give you an answer concerning this matter. If it be so, our God whom we serve is able to deliver us from the furnace of blazing fire; and He will deliver us out of your hand, O king. But even if He does not, let it be known to you, O king, that we are not going to serve your gods or worship the golden image that you have set up."

In other words, Nebuchadnezzar, whether or not God delivers us is not the issue. It is that he is there. And he loves us.

(Spoiler alert: although the men are tied up and cast into the fire, they suffer no harm. They are pulled out, clean and fresh, still trusting God. And, the text adds, Nebuchadnezzar lauds "their" God and orders that all his subjects worship this God instead. Read the full account in the second chapter of Daniel.)

It is, however, a complicated love. Many decades ago, I learned that a woman I knew in seminary had been diagnosed with inoperable brain cancer. Brenda would soon die. After I put down the letter in which I had read the news, I thought back to the Brenda I knew. She was a radical before her time. In a day when most ecclesiastical hierarchies, naturally filled with men, asserted that women could not serve as pastors, Brenda pushed back. Constantly. She insisted that women had as much call to be in pastoral ministry as did men. She believed that the church should open its eyes to the fullness of possibilities that women could bring to its pastoral workings. Although Brenda's teachers, and many of her male classmates, tried to dissuade her of her convictions (this was when the Christian feminist movement was just getting on its feet), Brenda held her ground. She firmly believed she was right.

(As things turned out, Brenda was prescient and, in my view, correct. Today, aside from a few Christian traditions that continue to impose boundaries on women in ministry, women are welcome to fully function in every type of Christian ministry endeavor. They are pastors, professors, administrators, priests, and more.)

Like radicals tend to do, Brenda made some people uncomfortable. The ugliest among my former male colleagues might therefore have argued that Brenda's premature demise was occasioned in part by the way that she allegedly undermined the teachings of the Bible. Although I cringe at the thought of someone taking this position (as I also cringed when I heard the late Jerry Falwell claim that AIDS was God's judgment on homosexuals), I recognize that it flows out of a different view of the activity of God. It flows out of a mindset that supposes it always knows exactly what God is doing, that thinks it always understands not just God's intentions but also what he does to bring the universe into alignment with those intentions. It's anything but humble. It misses the nuances, overlooks the corners.

It fails to see that divining the activity of God is a process rampant with ambiguity. It assumes that it always grasps what, in a world torn by competing pictures of divine favor, is good.

I prayed for Brenda often. Although I knew her prognosis was not favorable, I nonetheless believed that God could heal her. I also knew that God does not move mountains for everyone. So I prayed in a tension, the tension between the fact and love of God and the fact and bentness of a fallen world. I believed that anything was possible. I also believed that existence was capricious and terminal. I constantly juggled fact and feeling.

But as I told the person who let me know about Brenda, "I'd rather Brenda die in a world with value and meaning than not." Death in a senseless world is the worst death of all. Ask Camus's Meursault in *The Stranger*: he died never knowing quite why he was even alive in the first place.

On the other hand, about six years ago, one of my former sisters-in-law was diagnosed with a virulent form of stomach cancer. The doctors gave Debbie a few months. After extensive bible reading and prayer, however, Debbie became convinced that God wanted her to live. She came to believe that God would spare her and allow her to enjoy many more years on the planet. Debbie firmly believed she would be healed.

Unfortunately, Debbie did not heal. As the weeks went by, her condition grew worse. We prayed for her often. We wanted her to live. We wanted God to restore her to health. We wanted for Debbie to continue to enjoy her earthly existence. We wanted our feelings and belief to be one.

Two months after her diagnosis, however, as the doctors had predicted, Debbie died.

As she did, I thought about one of my aunts (another one of Mom's four sisters) who, at the age of seventy-five, was diagnosed with inoperable lung cancer and given only months to live. Although Aunt Kay was a believer she, unlike Debbie, took the news in stride. She accepted her mortality. She declined all treatments, deciding that they would just postpone the inevitable. She wanted only to go home and, as she put it, "die."

Once home, she wrote a letter to her twelve children. She urged them to be strong, to be happy about the life they had had with her, and to come to grips with the truth that her end was near. She closed the letter by saying, "Remember: always keep trying."

I loved Aunt Kay dearly. The home that she and Uncle Eddie shared in the pastoral hills of Lancaster County, Pennsylvania, west of Philadelphia, figured in many of my college travels, functioning as a sort of way station in my many hitchhiking trips across the country. As I stated in a note of condolence I sent her family after she passed, "I knew that wherever I had been and whatever I had become, whenever I was on the East Coast I would always have a 'Mom' to go to."

However, I realize that I will never be able to decide who made the best choice, Debbie or Aunt Kay. God works and God heals, yes, but who of us can say how he will do so?

Particularly if, as Rachel never tired of saying, God is always good.

Sometimes love's complexity boggles my mind.

In my first year of seminary, a visiting professor spoke

to one of my classes about Proverbs 2. The first two verses, he said, contain what he called "feminine" verbs. These urge the reader not to cry or call out to God for wisdom, but rather to be still and listen for it, to wait for him to speak it, to let God infuse her with wisdom as a river flows into the sea. To be open to whatever God—not she herself—might say to her.

The second two verses, he said, are "masculine" verbs. They advise the reader to call out, to cry loudly, to almost shout to God for wisdom. In contrast to the patient waiting the "feminine" verbs encouraged, these verbs, he said, counsel boldness. They urge the reader to step out and move aggressively to obtain the wisdom God has for her. Let nothing stand in the way, these verses counsel, of one's seeking the wisdom of God.

I have thought about this dichotomy countless times in the forty plus years since I heard this professor's message. And I haven't just thought about the content of what he said. I have also thought about how he closed his eyes when he was offering his perspective, how in spite of his knowledge and erudition he remained humble, even declining, as an Old Testament scholar, to speak about the notion of wisdom as it is presented in the New Testament. I remembered his kind manner, his glasses, his smile. To my youthful eyes, he was a paragon of virtue, a person who sincerely tried to live what he spoke.

This professor also told us that it was not as important to "know" the will of God as it was to be "in" the will of God. This was something new to me. As a person who had come to faith fairly recently, I had been conditioned by any number of teachers to suppose that my goal was to discern what God wanted me to do. What am I to do with the life before me? Or as one of my fellow camp counselors in East Texas asked the teacher at the beginning of a bible study on one particularly humid afternoon, "Do you have any helpful hints on knowing God's will"?

As I walked away from the visiting professor's lecture that November morning in Los Angeles, however, I resonated with the wisdom of what he was saying. As much as I wanted to know where God was directing me, that is, to know his "will" for me, I could now see that it was far more important that I "be" in his will. That I "be" in relationship with him. Even today, while I've certainly wished, indeed wished multiple times, that God would illumine my way with more clarity, I realize that this is not faith's point. Nor is it answered prayer. Some people come into distinctive callings; many more do not. Some people seem infused with God's power, some do not. Some people lose, some people gain. In every case, I'll never know or understand exactly why. Never. But I believe God is there. And despite the angst and heartbreak that the volatile tangle of life's unpredictability and God's mysterious ways unleash, that's all I really need to know.

As the late Thomas Merton, in a frequently cited phrase, once prayed, "My Lord God, I have no idea where I am going. I do not see the road ahead of me. I cannot know for certain where it will end."

But, I might add, "I believe that you, God, are there."

I cannot have it both ways. Either God is always there, or he is never there. There's no middle ground. With God there, I have questions yet not necessarily answers. If God is not there, however, I don't even have questions to ask.

Yes, I admit that faith appears to be highly irrational. Talking animals and ancient arks, vicious pillaging and unforgiving conquest, stoning for adultery and familial destruction for disobedience, angels and streets of gold: sometimes it's a hard pill to swallow. As it should be. Like it or not, faith is an eternal lens for a finite world. Questions are inevitable. But at least I can ask them.

Many years ago, I was backpacking out of Yosemite Valley, headed for Merced Lake and the high country that lay beyond it. It was a beautiful day in April: the sun was shining, the sky was blue, the meadows rippled with wildflowers. Yosemite's many waterfalls were bursting with energy, rushing madly over their crests of glaciated granite as they dropped into the Valley far below. And this being the Seventies, the last gasp of the countercultural movements of the Sixties, any number of men and women were stretching themselves out on the rocks along the trail, their tanned and, for the most part, unclad bodies catching, like lizards in a high desert, the warming rays of the spring sun. All was happy, all was good: it seemed as if life would always be effervescent and bright.

After reaching the top of the Valley, I camped for the night. I set up my tent along the Merced River which, at this point, was becoming Nevada Falls. All night I listened to the roar of Nevada's watery maelstrom, enraptured by its fierce glory, marveling as it barreled wildly and endlessly over the edge of the point to the Valley below. I heard it in my heart, I heard it in my dreams.

Come morning, I walked to the rim of the cliff, sat by the Falls and its screaming waters, and looked across the Valley. I saw Half Dome, I saw El Capitan. I saw the meadows, I saw the lakes. Then I looked at the Falls again. I could have watched for hours. And hours. I felt as if I were in a trance, captured and bound by the power of the water, woven into its innermost heart, falling madly, and blissfully, with it into the tranquil landscapes four thousand feet below me. As if I were witnessing a supernatural magic.

I was not a believer at the time. Indeed, I was very far from placing my trust in God. Or anything else, really, except for perhaps myself. As I watched the water, however, I felt as if, for a fleeting moment, I was looking into another world, a world beyond time and eternity, a world of unfettered harmony and peace, a world in which all was always well, a world in which I would find everything—and then some—I sought.

A world whose favor toward me had no limit.

Some years later, I was bicycling through the streets of Minneapolis with a friend with whose parents I was staying for the weekend. It was a beautiful day in the city, and thousands of people were outside, enjoying the near perfect summer weather. As we came to the end of our ride, we stopped at a waterfall, a waterfall my friend, Krista, particularly wanted me to see.

I soon realized why. Whereas in Yosemite I was at the top of the fall, here I was at the bottom. What a change. I found myself spellbound by the way the water slid over the overhanging rock, millions and millions of tiny droplets, dancing, prancing, happily frolicking in the afternoon sun. There seemed no end to its abundance, no end to its furious beauty, no end to its flawless enmeshment of ether and substance that sparkled so brilliantly in the golden light.

I felt as if this water was calling me, too, calling me to

join it, to step into its modulating suspension of space and time. To find peace, to encounter joy. To know favor and love forever.

All I had to do was believe it.

As we were driving home from dinner with some friends one night a number of years ago, Carol and I came to a railroad crossing whose barricades were about to fall and close the road to allow a train to pass. "I guess I should stop," I said.

"Go through it," Carol urged. So I did.

Almost immediately, flashing red lights appeared behind us. "Don't you know you're supposed to stop when you see a barricade coming down?" asked the police officer.

"I told him to do it," Carol said, "we just wanted to get through it."

To my surprise, the officer let me go. Did I deserve a ticket? Absolutely. Did I get a ticket? Definitely not. There was no reason for the officer to let me off, no reason for him to decline to cite me for a moving traffic violation. He had no legal incentive to let me go. But he did.

I had only to accept it. Much more recently, shortly after she began driving, Megan, like many a person her age, got a ticket. Subsequently, not wanting to taint her driving record with a traffic infraction, she, like most of us do, dutifully appeared for her day in court, hoping for leniency. At the stroke of 9:00 a.m., the judge walked into the courtroom, greeted the gathered assembly, and asked all defendants to get in a line before the "bench." Then, one by one, as each defendant came before him, he reviewed his or her case, taking, at most, two minutes to do so. In almost every instant, he dismissed all charges.

Megan's time was no different. Your charges will be dismissed, he told her. "Don't I need to go to traffic school?" Megan asked.

Smiling, the judge replied, "You can, but you don't need to."

"But won't doing that remove this charge from my record?" Megan responded.

Smiling once more, the judge said, "The charge is already gone."

Still not sure of what to think, Megan thanked the judge and left the bench. I was amused. Megan was given a gift, yes, but she wasn't sure that she could or should accept it. She had trouble believing it was true.

The waterfalls, whether in Yosemite or Minneapolis, were pure and unexpected delight. The officer letting me off was unexpected, too, a bit of joy on a winter evening. As was the judge dismissing Megan's charge: not what either of us had anticipated going into the courtroom. A gift.

Faith is a gift. But it is a gift that is hard to measure. Nearly twenty-five years ago, one of our neighbors was told he had non-Hodgkins lymphoma. For anyone who has been touched by cancer, whether directly or further afield, you know that this, unlike the lymphoma which hit Megan, is decidedly not curable. More often than not, it is a death sentence. Yet like most of us do when we receive a dire diagnosis, Chris resolved to fight it. He believed he could beat this cancer and move on with his life.

We all watched, trembling with hope. Initially, Chris seemed to get better. His energy levels increased, he became more active physically, and he began to talk more about life beyond the moment. When on occasion I walked across the street to visit with him, he was always upright, alert, and eager to converse about almost anything. As we both loved hiking in mountains and being in high places, whatever else we discussed, we usually found our way into talk of our alpine adventures. Chris talked about his travels in the Yukon, I my forays in the Brooks Range. We agreed that, in this life, mountains are surely one of the finest things.

We also talked of Chris's friend George. Although George at that time lived in Vancouver, he and Chris had shared many a wilderness escapade in years past. They loved each other dearly. Chris spoke frequently of his desire to reunite with George, to once more join mind and heart with him in blazing through a trackless wilderness. "When I get better," he often said, "I will."

We also discussed religion. One morning, we got into a conversation about the first part of one of my favorite verses from the gospel of John, 1:14, "And the Word (Jesus) became flesh and dwelt among us." Put another way, Jesus is God in human flesh. Although thinking about this verse rarely fails to move me, on this day, it seemed to move Chris even more. "Yes! That's it! Christ is God!" he suddenly cried out. "I see!"

"What do you see?"

"Me, you, God," he answered, "our lives in Jesus." I was amazed.

As the weeks continued, however, Chris began to decline. I no longer saw him as much: he was in intensive care in the hospital. Eventually, his wife Adelina brought him home, we all knew but did not say it, to die. That same night, I walked over to help her move Chris upstairs.

Though I saw him smile as broadly as ever, I could see that he was worse than I had ever seen him. It would not be long.

Two nights later, Chris died, passing away in Adelina's arms. It was awful. Adelina asked me to do the eulogy at the funeral. Standing at the pulpit of our town's Catholic church, I spoke of Chris's deep love of the outdoors and of some of his many adventures across the world. I also made mention of the morning we had talked about the incarnation and Chris's revelation about the beingness of God. I noted that in this I believed he had found a lasting love, an irresistibly gracious divine love. It was not a love he expected. Nor was it a love that, through much of his life, he had actively sought. Yet he had now come to believe it.

As people tend to do in these situations, everyone began to move on. Carol and I continued to reach out to Adelina and help however we could. One day, she told me, "How can I ever repay you?"

"It's grace," I replied, "all grace. You don't need to."

She couldn't believe it. She still doesn't believe in God, either. For Adelina, newly a widow at the age of forty-five, life soon became a zero sum game: it was her against the world. I have often felt sorry for her, alone as she is, missing Chris terribly, daily remembering and longing for the adventures they shared, never wanting, however, to believe in any measure of transcendent grace and meaning.

As I have said, I struggle with many aspects of Christian theology. I question the point of many doctrines, I crater when I contemplate the implications of the eternal verities of which they speak. I sometimes shudder when I consider the delicate character of the epistemological scaffolding upon which my relationship with God is built. Absolutely. But

I'm willing to let all this go for God's grace, his gracious sufficiency of point and purpose without boundary or proportion.

On the other hand, I struggle with grace. I struggle when I consider that, according to grace, a person can live all of her life rejecting God only to, on her deathbed, accept him, then be blessed in heaven with those who have followed God all their lives. I tremble when I hear that the person who ran our local park district's after school care for years and years, fervently loving every child who came her way, has died of a heart attack at the age of forty-six: what if she didn't believe in God? Then I turn around and see a person who insists he loves Jesus and looks forward to his "coming" express his anger that his taxes have been slightly raised to fund more programs for the poor. As Mahatma Gandhi is reported to have said, "I like your Christ, I do not like your Christians. Your Christians are so unlike your Christ."

Or as my Muslim friend Hashim often asks me, "How is it that Christians can believe in Jesus, not keep any of his commandments, then go to heaven, anyway?"

He has a good point: why? It's not sufficient to insist that, as many a Christian bumper sticker says, "I'm not perfect, just forgiven." While this may be theologically true, it does not augur well for anyone attempting to explain what seems to an outsider the abuse of divine grace. Or as German pastor and theologian Dietrich Bonhoeffer called it, "cheap grace."

It seems so Janusian.

A gracious God is often hard to see. And it's even harder to see when we try to disabuse ourselves of the notion that our efforts will make it otherwise. When God told

Abraham that he was be a father of many nations (Genesis 15), Abraham didn't ask what he should do or become to make this happen. He simply believed that it would take place. His only evidence for this, however, was God.

He at once had everything and nothing.

Over twenty years ago, when I was co-leading a high school youth group at my church, we decided, the Sunday before Earth Day, to highlight our charges' spiritual connections with the natural world by leading them in a hike in a nearby forest preserve. After walking for about twenty minutes on a path that wrapped around the pond in the middle of the preserve, we stopped to talk. As the day's teacher, I asked whether anyone had heard Joseph Haydn's "The Heavens are Telling [of the glory of God]."

No one responded affirmatively. I proceeded to say that it is based on the opening lines of Psalm 19, which read, "The heavens are telling of the glory of God, and their expanse is declaring the work of his hands. Day to day pours forth speech, and night to night reveals knowledge. There is no speech, nor are there words; their voice is not heard."

The imperative of survival is very much visible and present; divine grace and love are often not. We see them in shadows, shadows still struggling to make themselves known in full. In his *Lonely Man of Faith,* author Joseph Soloveitchik talks of what he calls the "untranslatability" of a personal experience of God. Maybe I can believe point, maybe I can believe purpose. Maybe I can believe grace. Maybe I will feel them, maybe I will not. As silent is the speech of heaven, so are the gifts that faith bequeaths. I often see them only in the effects they engender. I cannot measure ubiquity, I cannot measure infinitude. I cannot know fully how God's grace expresses itself in my reality. I can only believe it.

Grace is as beautiful as it is confounding.

Carol and I have known Ray and Barb for decades. For roughly half of those decades, Ray worked for a Christian apologetics organization in Dallas (the organization where, in fact, I met Carol). Barb mostly stayed home, watching their three children, and keeping active in neighborhood evangelism and good works. Ray and Barb lived on support, that is, they relied on the generosity of their fellow believers for donations to meet their monthly expenses.

Usually, they had enough. They never had a tremendous surplus, but they seemed to be able to cover essential expenses, and then some. About sixteen years ago, however, this changed. For a number of reasons, they had to leave the organization. After thinking and praying about it, they decided to establish a new ministry. Although some of their supporters stayed with them, many did not. Consequently, their income dropped dramatically. Every year, around Christmas, Ray sent out a prayer letter with news of their ministry along with a description of their most pressing financial needs, needs which their current income could not meet. These included dental work, doctor and hospital bills not covered by insurance, major automobile repairs, and the like. We found it rather depressing, really, that our friends were struggling so mightily. When we could, we sent them money.

One year, a couple of days after we received their annual missive, Ray called us. After some perfunctory conversation, he asked us for some money.

Responding that we will happy to send some, I added, "How long do you think you can keep living like this?"

"For as long as the Lord calls us to do it," Ray replied. "The Lord has been so good, so very good."

Even in the midst of some very difficult personal issues, Ray and Barb believed they experienced the gracious goodness of God. They believed they walked in the arms of God's grace. Empirically, of course, they could not prove it. That, however, is the tenuous path on which faith must tread: God's grace touches, yes, but it only really touches if it is believed. Grace will always be the hidden and unseen fact of divine favor. It is the "word without speech," the voice without sound: the certainty of the mystery.

As the years went by, Ray and Barb continued sending letters. Then they stopped. We soon learned why. Barb had been taken ill, ill in a life-threatening way. She was in hospice home care. It wouldn't be long. Though Carol and I didn't want to be judgmental, we couldn't help but think that her illness was due, in part, to her and Ray's many years of living with constant financial stress.

Even if they firmly believed that God had called them to this ministry. Fair enough: it's difficult to question another's sense of call. In addition, no call comes without its challenges. Perhaps these financial stresses were part of Ray and Barb's challenge. But an early death?

Always, however, Ray continued to say, "God has been so good." If I hadn't known better, I'd say he was being irrational. Ray was convinced, absolutely convinced, of God's presence and grace. His belief was unshakeable.

As things turned out, Barb didn't die. Within a year she was back to her former self. A year after that, however, she became sick again. Things did not go as well this time around. After a mercifully brief nadir, she died.

Ray was distraught. But, he said repeatedly, "I will trust God. He's always good."

Exactly what Rachel had always said. God is always good. All the time. His grace is constant and present. Even if we cannot see it. And even if, as we have seen in the case of Lou and Barb, nothing seems to work out as we would like it to.

How does one measure such things? Many centuries ago, as the armies of the Neo-Babylonian Empire approached Jerusalem, threatening it with annihilation, the prophet Habakkuk wrote, in the closing words of his prophecy to the city,

> "I heard [of the approach of Babylon] and my heart trembled at the Sound my lips quivered. Decay enters my bones and in my place I tremble, because I must wait quietly for the day of distress, for the people to arise who will invade us. Though the fig tree should not blossom and there be no fruit on the vines, though the yield of the olive should fail and the fields produce no food, though the flock should be cut off from the fold and there be no cattle in the stalls, yet I will exult in the Lord, I will rejoice in the God of my salva- tion." (Habakkuk 3:16-18)

Even in the face of personal destruction, Habakkuk remained confident in the fact of God, certain of his grace and purpose. Regardless of what happened, he would retain his trust in the goodness and purpose of God. Habakkuk knew that God's gift was more than an improvement in circumstance, more than an upturn in fortune, more than divine whimsy. He knew that because, as the psalmist proclaims, the whole earth is God's, there is nowhere in the universe where God's favor is not present, nowhere on the planet in which God's love and grace cannot be found. Divine magnanimity and purpose pervade every part of reality.

And he would trust it.

Many times I have heard people say that, "But by the grace of God, there go I." More often than not, people state this when they hear of another person who is experiencing significant difficulty, hardship, or pain, and they are not. It is by God's grace, they are opining, that they do not find themselves in a similar predicament.

Really? This reduces grace to a measurement of how comfortable, at a given moment, we are. It assesses results, not meaning. Are there levels of God's grace? Does God parse out who he is or how he expresses himself?

Hardly. Although when we view their lives through an "earthly" lens, we may suppose that some believers have "better" lives, materially, emotionally, or spiritually than others, I am loath to say that their lives are necessarily "better." Better to whom: humans or God? And how do we define "better"?

God is not a measure. God is presence. God is not necessarily success, worldly or otherwise, and he's not necessarily, in worldly terms, failure. God is infinite grace moving in a finite reality. He is a mark of eternity in a temporal realm, a voiceless eternality of speech that exceeds present cacophony. I cannot divide, parcel, or allocate him. In addition, while I may be able, theologically speaking, to define God's grace, I really cannot: always and always, regardless of the circumstance or situation, grace is God's fullness. It is who God is.

As Habakkuk said, faith is trusting in hidden certainty. The hidden certainty of God and his love for me. It is, as Psalm 37 puts it, to feed "securely" on God's faithfulness, to feed on the simple yet incredibly profound "thereness" of God. Nothing more, nothing less.

Even in the blackest darkness.

As things went, the Neo-Babylonian army did indeed enter Jerusalem, destroy its temple, and ship thousands of its people to Babylon. It was a debacle of unspeakable proportion. Wandering through the ruined city, Jeremiah wrote, in the opening lines of his book of Lamentations, "How lonely sits the city that was once full of people. She who was once great among the nations is now a widow; she who once walked with princes has been reduced to being a forced laborer." One of the grandest cities in the ancient world had been reduced to rubble.

Yet Jeremiah also writes that God's faithfulness "is new every morning, great [oh Lord] is your faithfulness" (Lamentations 3:22). Regardless of what has happened, God and his grace remain. That's the hope, that's the reality.

If you believe it.

When I began seminary, though I was thoroughly psyched for the opportunity to study the Bible in an academic setting, I did, as I briefly mentioned earlier, endure much in terms of financial hardship. I struggled constantly to make ends meet. I considered a quarter as gold. A dollar was Fort Knox. Throughout my four years in seminary, a lovely elderly couple faithfully sent me $15.00 every month. "We're happy to do it," they always said, "it's only fifteen dollars."

Maybe for you, I thought! For me, fifteen dollars was a vast sum. Once told that a repair I needed for my car would cost me $100.00, I freaked. "That's a lot of dough," I said.

Indeed.

Although I worked part-time, the money I brought in never seemed to be enough. Between a car payment (an arrangement into which I somewhat naively entered as I was closing out my time in Henderson, Texas, an experience which I describe in greater detail below), auto insurance, rent, food, gasoline (which was, at that time, thanks to the recent OPEC engineered quadruple increase in the price of oil, rather high relative to my income), and other necessities, I struggled to finish a month in the black.

Sometimes I did not. To enlarge on a story I mentioned earlier, I recall waking up one spring morning to look at my bank account and see that I was literally down to my last dollar. I had exactly $1.35 to my name.

What was I going to do? Of course, I prayed, and of course I asked others to pray for me. And of course I tried to hope in God, to believe in his faithfulness to me, to believe in the fact of his grace. But nothing changed. At the end of the day, even the end of the week, I still did not know how I would have the money I needed to eke out even a semblance of "civilized" existence.

On this, I was not encouraged to be told that compared to billions of other people in the world, I was, by gosh, rich: I had far more than these billions of others would ever have. Although this may have been literally true, I was not living where these people lived. I was living in the wealthy, fat, and sassy United States of America. We made more money, yes, but we had to spend more to fund our life necessities. It was relative.

Oh, I was occasionally told during this time, "The Lord provides." This I did not dispute. I wanted to believe God was faithful and good; I really did. I wanted to believe God would not let me down, that he would not abandon me. But I struggled with understanding how. How would I see God's love and grace and presence?

Yet within a week I had more than enough money to meet my expenses, more money than I could ever earn in my part-time job. I knew the money didn't appear magically, yet I also knew that I could not definitively prove God had provided it. And I knew that it was too facile to conclude that I was experiencing "more" grace than I had before. That's a dead end answer.

I had to tumble blindly into the gaping maw of faith.

A few paragraphs ago, I noted that I had worked at a community action agency in East Texas. You may or may not know that, culturally, East Texas was, at that time, very much like the so-called Deep South. It was a place deeply divided by race, a region in which racism bloomed openly and, sometimes, with a high level of confidence and widespread social approval. For a life long liberal like me, it was a frustrating land in which to work and find a home.

But work I did. Perhaps I worked too hard. Within a

year, the county commissioners decided that it no longer wanted our agency in town. We were "stirring up too much stuff," they said. In other words, we were doing too much to empower the town's African-American community. I suppose they had a point. After all, we funded daily lunches for African-American elderly; a summer lunch program for African-American youth; a legal aid clinic (which ended up serving whites as well as blacks); a Head Start program; and various development projects in the impoverished areas—always African American—of the counties we served. Yet we did so because even after over a hundred years after the end of the Civil War, black people in East Texas were still shut out of the economic mainstream.

As tensions between the agency and the commissioners mounted and tempers on both sides flared, the federal agency which oversees all community action agencies came to town. As its people investigated the matter, I felt increasingly under fire. My boss, the executive director, resigned; other staff members left shortly thereafter. Although I loved what I was doing, I came to conclude that I could no longer do it effectively. I decided to resign, too.

One day, before I decided to resign, I was out bicycling, enjoying the breezy warmth of a spring morning and thinking about my life. As I tooled through the rambling countryside of pale blue lakes and galloping stretches of pine trees that spread out from Henderson, I prayed. "God," I said, "I'm willing to give up this job if it's what you want me to do. I'm willing to let it go. I'm willing to let it go even if I do not have an inkling what I will do next."

At that time, I was twenty-three years old. Surrendering everything to God's grace at that point was therefore easy.

I had my life ahead of me. I had plenty of time to regroup and move on. Untethered to a mortgage, without intimate personal attachments, I could easily let go.

If I were to fast forward forty-five years, however, I must admit that letting go is immeasurably more difficult. So much more, it seems, is at stake; so much more, it seems, can be lost. Furthermore, given my struggles with seminary penury, I don't know that it's necessarily easier to trust God when one has very little. Either way, I wrestle with its measure. How does one measure, and trust, the invisible presence of God?

As we saw earlier, God will not restore everyone to health. And he's not likely to bring a deceased loved one back from the dead. Moreover, if the company for which a believer works has gone bankrupt and she has lost her job, perhaps her dream job, God will probably not intervene in the global economic system to restore the company back to life. Furthermore, as we have also observed, if either through an accident or natural causes a believer has lost the use of one or more of her limbs, God will probably not divinely rejuvenate her body.

It's convoluted, so terribly convoluted, this wonderful and overwhelming fact of God's presence of love and grace. I earlier mentioned my friend Dave, who lost all his appendages in a mountaineering accident. If one day a medical breakthrough resulted in Dave's appendages being restored, would I say that *this* is God's grace in faithfulness? That Dave simply had to continue to believe that relief would, even after many years, come?

It's impossible to say.

Once again, it comes down to the issue of belief. If

I believe, I trust. And if I trust, I believe. But this is not always a comfort when I am stuck in the darkness: I'm still foundering on the rocks of unresolved causation.

Yet this is not faith's issue. It is rather to understand that although I may wish for evidence, I may not get it. It is to perhaps hope for proof, but also to acknowledge that it may not see it in full. Although my faith is, necessarily, based on reason, its validation, as circular as this sounds, is itself. It cannot be otherwise. If I can see, I do not need faith.

Faith is not sight. It's faith (look at 2 Corinthians 5:7).

This may seem flippant, it may seem juvenile. It may seem inordinately foolish. In a sense, it is. Faith is indeed foolish. It will not always make earthly sense. But it will always make eternal sense.

Many years ago, some missionary friends of mine, a family of five working in a small African country, saw, as they looked out their window one afternoon, four opponents of their work, armed to the hilt, approaching their house. They immediately fled to a back room. Unfortunately, all that separated that room from the front room, the room into which the attackers entered, was a glass door. My friends would be, so the saying goes, sitting ducks. There seemed no escape.

Then the most remarkable thing happened. The four men walked directly to the glass door and looked through it. My friends could see every crease in their faces, every flash of anger in their eyes. Yet the men did nothing. It was as if, my friends shared with me, they "didn't see us."

My friends remained in that house for twenty more years. In time, their ministry came to bear more fruit than they had dared imagine. And that was just what they could see. Their decision to enter that small African country without any armed protection would seem to many people the most foolish of choices. But my friends weren't thinking of the present. They were thinking of eternity.

Theirs was the foolishness of a faith that believes when everything suggests it should not.

In 1956 an American missionary named Jim Elliot, with four other male missionaries, decided, after three years of living in the jungles of eastern Ecuador, to initiate contact with the Auca (now Huaroni) Indian tribe. They hired a plane to drop them off on the edge of Huaroni territory and waited. Sadly, the Huaronis, likely not fully understanding the nature of the missionaries' overture, quickly killed all five men. When news of the deaths hit the news, people around the world wondered why these Americans, some of whom were married with young children, would take this kind of risk. Couldn't they have found a better way to establish a line of communication with a tribe known for its hostility to outsiders? It seemed the height of foolishness, a pernicious, misguided decision of faith.[6]

Put another way, God is a lunatic.

Three years later, Elliot's widow, Elisabeth, went to live with the Huaronis. Subsequently, many members of the tribe, including the men who had killed Jim, converted to Christianity. Multiple apologies and acts of forgiveness

---

[6] As many people did more recently when an American named Jonathan Chau, inspired to share the gospel with an isolated tribe on an island in the Philippines, a tribe known for its enmity to outsiders, clandestinely and, as it turned out, illegally, paid some people to take him to that island so that he could speak to them. Almost immediately after he set foot on the beach, he was shot full of arrows and died. He was twenty-six years old.

followed. The transformation was extraordinary. There was no earthly reason for Elliot and his comrades to contact a hostile tribe. There was no earthly reason for the Huaronis to welcome Elliot's widow, much less to come to believe in her God. None at all. Faith isn't about the seeing of the moment. It's about the seeing of forever.

Roughly a year after Jim's death, Elisabeth published a book, *Through Gates of Splendor.* In poignant yet straightforward prose, she told her and Jim's story, how they met, how they got married, how they decided to go to Ecuador, and how Jim and his comrades made the decision to go to the Huaronis. Elisabeth filled her narrative with quotes from her late husband's journals. One line has resonated with many generations of evangelicals. It is, "He is no fool who gives what he cannot keep to gain that which he cannot lose."

Precisely. If God didn't exist, faith is risible. Even though God does exist, however, faith remains baffling. It often raises far more questions than answers. For the rest of my days, I am left to wonder why my missionary friends' trust in God resulted in a positive earthly outcome, and in the case of Jim Elliot, a decidedly negative one.

Eternity's silence can be deafening.

But it's heard. Ray and Barb heard it. Jim Elliot heard it. Chris and Dave heard it, too. Chris found it in the months and months he struggled to orient himself to the implications of his paralysis; Dave found it in the hospital as he recovered from hours of multiple surgeries.

The music is playing.

And it's always playing for more than the moment.

Toward the close of his letter to the church in the

bustling ancient city of Ephesus, Paul describes God's love as something that "surpasses" knowledge (Ephesians 3:19). It is a love, he says, that, try as we might, we will never fully understand. It is unfathomable. But it's there.

As to precisely *how* it's there, well, that is the unresolvable question.

Consider Paul's words in the eighth chapter of his letter to the church at Rome,

> "For I am convinced that neither death, nor life, nor angels, nor principalities, nor things present, nor things to come, nor powers, nor height, nor depth, nor any other created thing, will be able to separate us from the love of God, which is in Christ Jesus our Lord." (Romans 8:38-39)

Although many believers, including me, find these verses singularly comforting and inspiring, I also acknowledge that, from one standpoint, at least for me, they do not. I still face the silence. The silence of grace, the silence of eternity: the silence of the love of God. Yes, as I have noted previously, I see, in the historical person of Jesus, tangible expression of God's love. After all, Jesus is hard to miss. But now Jesus is gone. God is no longer physically present. All I therefore have are records of memories of what once was, memories of a love that exceeded all boundaries, all limits, all sensibilities.

On the other hand, as musician Richard Wagner once observed, perhaps the inexpressible can only speak to us in secrecy, the secret intimacies of our heart.

Furthermore, if God's grace shouted into life and went mute at death, it would be as hollow as the temporality in which I had known it. If, on the other hand, God's grace said nothing in life then erupted in song at death, it would not be true, either. Only in grace's present silence do I see it fully, see it, necessarily, as belief in the mute ubiquity of divine favor. Even when one day in the future I step into the other side of faith and experience the voice of the silence with which I have walked in my days of temporal sojourn, what will be brightening my world will not necessarily be love or grace but rather, in a word, God.

Everything else will follow.

In the end, it is therefore about "eventually." Such a slippery word. Eventually is a word that can cover, no pun intended, a multitude of sins. It is a word that can mean something will happen in a few minutes; it is a word that can mean something will happen in a few years. Or in several lifetimes. Eventually is a word that one can use to justify almost anything about the activity of God. As Bach's "Mein Gott, wei lang, ach lange" says, "My God, how long, oh, how long? Too great is my distress. No end do I see to sorrow and care."

On the other hand, as parts of numerous psalms (27:14; 40:4; 127:5 to name a few) attest, there is no other way to frame it. Sure, as I have already said, I can say that I have believed in and walked with God long enough to persuade me that, in everything that happens, he is with me. That he is steadfastly working in the circumstances of my life for my good, day by day conforming me more fully to the image of Jesus. After over forty-five years, it's almost automatic.

On the other hand, although this reflex may be

"automatic," it is far from easy. I frequently need to overlook the fact of everything to affirm the fact of everything. Or as "Mein Gott" adds, I must set aside the immediate and "Cast myself, oh my heart, into the loving arms of God." It's mindbending, it's paradoxical. Yet how else am I to believe?

Toward the close of a 2013 debate he had with mathematician John Lennox about the existence of God, outspoken atheist Richard Dawkins remarked, "After all this, it all comes down to the resurrection. It seems so parochial."

Dawkins was responding to how Lennox had noted in his closing arguments that without the resurrection, Christianity would not mean much. For all the wonderful words that Jesus spoke, if he had died and never returned, history would remember him as just one more itinerant sage who, for a season, persuaded people to think differently about things big, broad, and eternal. While those who survived him would have been free to remember and attempt to live by what Jesus had said, they would have been acutely aware that his words were, in the end, just that: words. Words without any power or agency other than the charisma and wisdom of the one who was recorded as saying them. Jesus would be a first century version of the Buddha (except that the Buddha didn't die on a cross).

What complicates this apologetic is that, outside of the biblical account, we have no other records of Jesus rising from the dead. Not that I do not believe the biblical accounts are true; much research indicates that they are. Nonetheless, they remain accounts written by people who believed the resurrection actually happened. Impartial historiography they are not.

It seems a slender point to which to cling.

But it stands. Earlier I mentioned our friend Vera, dying at the age of ninety, sure she was going into another, more glorious life. At her funeral, the officiating minister read from letters which Vera's two sons had written to her after she passed. In his letter, Paul, one of her two sons, wrote of how much he loved her and how much he will miss her. He closed by saying, "I know I will see you, Mom, in heaven."

Could Paul know? Only in his faith.

About five years ago, I got a call from one of my aunts (in truth, Jeanne was not a "blood" aunt, but rather a long time friend of the family who had "adopted" my siblings and me as her nieces and nephews) in Los Angeles. Her doctors, she said, had just told her that the cancer which she had beaten back three times before had resurfaced, this time with an unstoppable malevolence. They had given her three weeks. I immediately made plans to fly to California for the weekend. Bob came out, too, and the two of us spent much of Saturday sitting with Jeanne as she lay on a hospital bed that had been brought into her apartment. We talked, we laughed. And we remembered. We remembered all the good times we had together, the times we spent exploring art museums in Los Angeles; attending family reunions in northern Michigan; sightseeing in Chicago; and much more. It was lovely but heartbreaking.

But Jeanne remained strong, stronger than Bob or I. For many years leading up to this day, she and I had talked about faith in God. Although she had once been rather nominal about her belief, as she had moved into her sixties, Jeanne "rediscovered" the beauty of a life devoted to trusting God. We often talked about God and theology for hours.

Now, however, we were both standing at the precipice. There was no escape. If we really believed in God and his eternity, we now had to own it, own our faith absolutely and fully. No more excuses, no more running: this was the ultimate test of our willingness to trust. Before I left for the airport on Sunday, I visited Jeanne one last time. "I'll see you again," I said, "I'll see you again."

She smiled. She knew.

Did I? Never had my faith seemed so opaque and indecipherable. I felt as if I was flying blind: liminality was hanging on a string.

But that, I reminded myself, is faith.

Roughly five years before I bid Jeanne farewell, I watched Mom take her last breath. I watched her slowly fade into the finality of earthly existence, her tiny body sliding into material oblivion as she lay on her bed in the bedroom in the home in which she had lived for over fifty years. "Do I really believe that Mom will rise?" I said to myself, "do I really believe that I will see Mom again? Do I really believe in resurrection?"

Do I really believe that, as Paul averred, "To live is Christ, to die is gain" (Philippians 1:21)?

Only if I've surrendered myself to it. A couple of weeks after I had come to believe in the fact and person of Jesus, and still living in the forest outside Jasper, I still wasn't sure what I had done. One day, a day on which the first snows had mantled the mountains that ringed the camp, however, I felt convicted that because faith is, in its deepest moments, trust, I needed to step beyond just assenting to belief. I needed to act on it. I had been thinking about the last person who had talked to me about Jesus, a guy about my age who one weekend had come to the camp from his mother's home in Edmonton, a five hour drive east on Canadian highway 16. "You've got to give your faith your all, Billy," Eric said before he left, "you've got to let nothing stand in the way. Jesus demands everything."

Frightening? Absolutely. Necessary? So it seemed. Nonetheless, I struggled. One day, however, I decided I was ready. After I ate some breakfast and pulled myself away from the campfire (morning temperatures were dipping into the thirties), I headed toward the trail to Old Fort Point. Sitting about a thousand feet above the camp, Old Fort Point provides a spectacular view of the entire Jasper area, from the boreal hinterlands to its north to the massive edifice of Mt. Edith Cavell (named after a World One battlefield nurse who tended to all whom she encountered, be they German, English, or French, and who was eventually captured and executed by the forces of the Kaiser) looking south. Glorious during daylight hours, the Point's view took on surreal tones when darkness fell, Jasper and its mountains rising and falling together under millions and millions of stars. "Like a cartoon," one of my fellow campers once said.

There was no one else on the Point that morning. It was just me and the mountains. And God. How odd, I thought. One day I didn't believe; the next day I did. In the space of a slim moment, a wisp of nocturnal time, I had totally revised my epistemological categories. I embraced a belief I had long despised, and discarded years and years of skepticism and repugnance: I admitted to the reality of the supernatural. I had asserted that what I had never imagined could exist in personal form now did, and that which I had once cavalierly ground into the dust of high mountains and countercultural fervor now suddenly, and unexpectedly, stood before me, its truth more powerful and compelling than anything I had ever experienced before.

All in the span of a moment. I knew so very little about being a "Christian." I knew nothing about the Bible, I knew nothing about attending church, I knew nothing about prayer. But I sensed that the euphoria of my "night with Jesus" would probably not last. Moreover, I was well aware that I couldn't stay in the mountains indefinitely. Life was tightening its grip. The rest of my years, whatever they might look like, were calling.

What I also knew was something which I have spent the last forty-six years trying to grasp: faith is not being able to know fully. If I had known what I would be on the other side of my conversion experience, would I still have entered into it? I had no idea.

Yes, I had found Jesus. Yes, I felt renewed and remade in ways I could not have imagined. But did I trust Jesus as more than a belief? And did I have any idea what this meant?

So many questions. And no one to answer them. But even with the very limited knowledge I then possessed of Christianity, I understood that, all things considered, I was fundamentally looking at an issue of security. I was trying to determine whether I could, on a long term basis, find security in something *without* security, yet something which nonetheless seemed to have had, in one fateful night, transformed everything I was.

I didn't know what to do. Thinking about my childhood in the Catholic Church, however, I decided that if I were to talk to God, I should kneel. So I got on my knees and said,

"Oh God, I give all of myself to you. I don't want to hold anything back. I place my life in your hands. Absolutely. Forever and ever."

And that was that.

Barely three weeks later, I returned to my camp after a day of hiking to find that someone, a person who had been staying at the camp, had, while we (about six of us were still living at the camp) were all gone, absconded with a great deal of our equipment. I no longer had a tent. Some of my warmest outerwear was gone, too. Sooner than I had anticipated, I had to think about leaving the mountains. My dream was over.

As a friend of mine in seminary said when, years later, I recounted this incident to her, "It didn't take long."

No, it did not. It did not take long for me to have opportunity to experience the limits to which I was willing to surrender to, and trust, God. Here I was, barely a month into my new journey with Jesus, and I had just been relieved of some of my most treasured worldly possessions. Even though I believed in God.

It's funny. I didn't get angry at God. Maybe I didn't know I could! I didn't cry, either: what would be the point? I knew I'd never see those things again. And I certainly didn't pray. Despite my morning on the Point, I still wasn't sure I knew how.

I just accepted it. Yet whenever I had in the past encountered other rather insuperable problems, be they in politics, culture, or my mountain travels, I had done exactly the same. I accepted it and went on. What was different now?

I didn't know. I absolutely didn't know. All I knew was that I had to start making plans to leave Jasper.

"I don't like the word 'surrender'." My sister Kathleen's spouse, Kirsten, told me this as we talked one afternoon in her family's cabin on the shores of Huntington's Lake in the Sierra Nevada. Kathleen, Ellen, and I had just returned from a wonderful four day backpack in the Sierra. We had undertaken the trip at Kathleen's request: it was how she wanted to celebrate her sixtieth birthday. (Regrettably, because he had slipped on some ice the previous winter and suffered a concussion, brother Bob didn't think he was ready for the altitude we would encounter, and stayed at home.). It was a lovely four days: flawless weather, gobs of wildflowers (which, like their mother, Ellen and Kathleen carefully noted in their flower book), uniformly remarkable vistas of peak, lake, meadow, and sky. We reveled.

At night, although per wilderness regulations for the upper altitudes we could not build a campfire, the three of us sat together and talked. I told stories of my previous backpacks on nearby trails; Ellen talked about her husband, Daniel, and their recent trip to see their son in Brazil (where he was living with his girlfriend); and Kathleen read a few passages from a book she had brought. The author of this book, who was looking for spiritual wholeness, talked of how he bounced from the Bible to I Ching symbol to Jewish Kabbalah to Hindu meditation, only to find that, today, he was still looking. It was an apt volume for the trip. Stars filled the skies every night. If we stayed out long enough, we saw the Milky Way.

Like the writer of Kathleen's book, Kirsten has devoted her life to finding her spiritual center. She works diligently at it, attending lectures and retreats, reading constantly, and engaging in a wide range of spiritual practices. But, she made clear to me that day, she wants to find whatever she finds, herself, on her own power and initiative: she doesn't want help or input from God. She would rather keep wandering—and happily so—than surrender her individual sovereignty to an invisible deity.

I certainly understood. Surrender is hard. And unnerving. After I left Jasper, I hitchhiked to Eric's mother's home in Edmonton. I arrived very late at night. Not wishing to disturb anyone, I laid out my sleeping bag on the back porch. Eric and I connected the next morning. "You surrendered, Billy," he said, "and God opened doors for you. You're safe here."

So much to think about. In talking with Eric later that morning, however, I began to see some clarity. At least in part. I knew that it was for the hope of abundance that I had believed in Jesus. And that it was for the felt imperative of commitment that I subsequently surrendered to him. Yet it was trust that sustained both. I could not have abundance without trust. Yet I would not trust unless I believed that abundance was on the other side. And I would only surrender if I had both. Faith only made sense when all three experiences, abundance, surrender, and trust, mesh together.

Even if, at that point, I still had no idea of what it all meant.

Earlier that fall, just about a week after I came to faith, I had traveled to Edmonton to visit Eric for a few days. He was of course thrilled that I had come to believe in Jesus. The second afternoon we were together, he played for me Johnny Cash's latest album. It was a selection of songs in which "the

Man in Black" celebrated his return to committed faith in Jesus. One of the songs was a John Denver composition, "Follow Me." A line in its second stanza stuck with me. It was Denver's wish that he would like to share his life with whomever he was singing to, that he would always like to have this person beside him. Such would be his greatest joy. As Eric played the song, played it over and over and over, I let myself imagine that Denver's words were those of God. That God was singing to me, that he was telling me that he wanted to follow me, that he wanted to always be with me, that he wanted always to share his abundant life with me. That he wanted to grow old with me.

If I followed him.

Jasper now well behind me, I left Eric's house the next day to hitchhike to Saskatchewan. Not much time passed before a massive rig of a truck stopped. Its driver was going "down the road a bit, to Winnipeg." Perfect. It was an odd ride, however. The driver soon announced that he had to make a furniture delivery along the way. Would I like to help him for some extra cash?

Sure. But when we had finished, the driver got his rig back on the highway, pulled off at the nearest truck stop and took a lengthy nap. It was very late that night when I showed up at the home of Tom, a guy I had met in Waterton National Park some months before, and who was now living with his parents in Saskatoon. His mom graciously took me in, and I stayed a few days with them. I also celebrated my birthday. Did I find abundance? Hard to say. Regardless, I would not have found anything had I not put out my thumb on the edge of Edmonton a few days before.

Then I headed south to Regina, where I bumped into a

Christian, Everett, who told me, "Billy, you say you found Jesus. I believe you have. Now you really have two choices: to stay or not. There's no middle ground. You said you found Jesus' abundance; I say that you have only found its key."

It's a funny sort of abundance. It's an abundance that, in the lens of faith, I will only experience if, and only if, I decide that nothing else, absolutely nothing else in this life, will provide similarly.

Such a big "if." At the end of my summer as a camp counselor in East Texas (a position I accepted after resigning my post at the community action agency), having already applied for admission to a seminary in Los Angeles, I took a chance and made plans to drive to California. After making an overnight stop with some friends in Dallas, I drove north to Colorado. I wanted to see mountains again. It had been two years since I had set foot in the heights. I wondered whether I'd be able to; I wondered whether God would allow me to experience such joy.

As I drove out of Denver, then through Boulder, getting ever closer to the entrance of Rocky Mountain National Park, the front range of Rockies suddenly came into my view, glistening in the morning light. I wept. How could such marvel be?

As I remember this moment today, I realize I would be hard pressed to parse the layers of this joy, that is, to decide which were of God and which were of, well, me. It's my belief. I believe that because I have committed myself to God and that, consequently, he is moving in my heart and life, any joy that I experience comes, ultimately, from his activity in me. But someone else, someone who does not believe in God, could experience the joy of mountains—and

I have seen countless unbelievers do so over the years—and conclude that it is of her and only her, the expression of her life experience at that particular moment. Who is to say? It really comes down to belief. Because I believe, I attribute this joy, at least in part, to God. But that's just me.

And my history with God.

Compounding my dilemma is the ethereal nature of joy. Deep joy, be it of God or not, is, in many ways, an experience of the whole person: everything about us is participating in it. We cannot possibly separate it from who we are. If I therefore believe that God is working in every part of me, and I do, I must also realize that I will never know, never know precisely how this will be. While I can say that my joy, whatever the experience that occasioned it may be, is of God, I still cannot know where "I" stop and God begins. Nor should I even try: it's like trying to separate water from water. Not that God and I are ontologically one of course, just that as we cannot parse joy, so we cannot differentiate it, either.

Again, however, I say this only because I believe. Ironically, this is at once the problem *and* the solution. It affirms me, it affirms God. Only, however, if both are true.

In the four days I roamed through the park, I continued to rejoice, amazed and grateful that I was here. The sunrise in the fog over a peak, the lichen covered rocks and flower dappled meadows, the steely blue shine of alpine lakes, the profusion of stars: it was all so very astonishing. I liked to think that such astonishment was of God, that my feelings of rapture were the fruit of my faith in a living and personal transcendent presence. That it reflected a deep union with God.

That had I not believed in God, I would not have experienced it at the level I was. But how could I know? It's a very delicate line. As Sherrill from Jasper once wrote to me, "It's a fine world we live in. Let's enjoy it." Absolutely. We do live in a marvelous world. From Sherrill's standpoint, however, it is a world whose abundance is all the abundance we will ever have.

God's not an issue.

What then is this abundance, this abundance whose promise changed my life, this abundance that claims it is greater than anything earthly, this abundance that although it is very much present, asserts itself to be nonetheless tethered to an eternal presence beyond it? Though the evidences of its materiality seem real, at least to me, its larger tracks are nowhere to be found.

Except by faith.

I've already mentioned my experience at the community action agency in Texas and how I had to let go of everything I knew when I resigned without a job prospect in sight. I also mentioned Megan's cancer. I might also note, considerably more recently, when I was informed that, due to declining enrollment and "institutional contraction," the teaching position that I had held for nearly twenty years, a position in which I was told repeatedly I was tenured, was to be eliminated at the end of the current academic year. Or when, my first year of seminary, while in trying to make ends meet by delivering newspapers (the *Los Angeles Times*) in the early hours of the morning, I was accosted by two men who, at knifepoint, stole my car. Or one July while I was backpacking with Payson and he being only twelve years old at the time, I woke in the middle of the night in our isolated near timberline camp to hear a mountain lion rampaging through the surrounding forest. Or many years before that night, waking up in the early morning in the sparsely traveled Beartooth Mountains in southern Montana to hear a grizzly bear growling and sniffing outside my tent.

Or about seven years ago being told by our insurance company that Carol's car, a car that she dearly loved, was, as a result of Payson rear ending it into another vehicle, totaled, forcing us to buy another one much earlier than we had planned. The list goes on and on and on, really, as it should. Such is the way of life in a broken world. In every instance, I had two choices as to how I might respond: anger, bitterness, and frustration, or equanimity, surrender, and trust. Moreover, regardless of which I chose, my situation might not change appreciably. I still might not have a clear path forward.

On the other hand, these choices would stand whether God existed or not. Humanness creates them, but only belief divides them.

Not to say that I didn't ever get sad or angry. One doesn't take the loss of a vehicle lightly, nor does one quite know how to compose oneself when a mountain lion or grizzly bear is roaming through one's camp. What rings most true is that although I certainly felt fright, isolation, grief, and loss in these situations, I chose to trust the abundance. I chose to trust that God's abundance, however I could define or grasp it, was greater than the moment. I chose to elevate indefinability over definition, chose to privilege invisibility over physical presence.

Put another way, I traded what I knew to be broken for

what I believed to be not. Though I couldn't see the finished product, I believed that it was, in incipient form, there.

It's a terrible tension, really, a terribly wonderful tension. It talks of the planet's life, it announces its end. It upholds evanescence, it proclaims eternity. It notes present anguish; it looks to future joy. Faith's tapestry is incomprehensible.

That's why it's difficult.

In his *Dark Night of the Soul,* the Spanish mystic John of the Cross writes of his desire to divest himself of all semblance of self and worldly desire, to excise everything that is "him" so that God can fully dwell in him. He longs to submit, absolutely and completely, to the will of God. He wants nothing in him to mar or interfere with his pursuit of his creator.

It is the most arduous of surrenders, one that occasions lost as much as found: an *ascent* into the valley of death.

Such an ascent is, however, as author Shelden Vanauken put it in his biography of C. S. Lewis, one of "severe mercy." As we observed in our brief look at *Hind's Feet in High Places,* God's mercy does not always come easily. But this is what faith necessitates and demands. Although the divide between belief and disbelief may be linguistically slender, in terms of how we know, it is unspeakably vast. Faith's inescapabilty is exceeded only by its unfathomability: how else can we measure it but by our faith in that to which it points?

And that to which it points is, for now, not fully known to us. We're still trapped, to quote Paul again, "in a riddle."

Many years ago, I was sitting with Megan in the bathroom of our condominium in Hyde Park on the south side of Chicago, standing duty while she was using a "real" toilet. We had been working toward this moment for a couple of months, Carol and I coaxing, guiding, encouraging Megan to abandon her little potty and "graduate" to the real deal (as it were). We had come a long way since the afternoon when, as I sat in our sunroom that overlooked the street, Megan walked up to me and said, "I'm going to stand next to you and go poop."

As we looked at each other in the bathroom that night, Megan suddenly said to me, "Daddy, I want to accept Jesus right now!"

I was thrilled. I had been talking to her about Jesus since the day she was born. We had read books about Jesus, we had listened to cassette tapes about Jesus, we had heard sermons and Sunday school lessons about Jesus. For better or worse, in terms of religion, Jesus was all Megan had known. Jesus changed my life; I wanted Megan to have the same experience. Not that Jesus would change Megan's life in the way he had changed mine; she was only three years old. But he would change it.

In contrast, brother Bob and his wife Jill raised their children, three boys, without religion or any talk of God. They taught their boys to view life in material terms only (although as I pointed out earlier, Michael, their oldest, did, in his mid-twenties, come to believe in Jesus, and now attends a Greek Orthodox church). I could say the same about a few of the people who attend my atheist discussion group: they have been raised totally devoid of talk of formal spirituality or God.

While I therefore point to the "riddle" in which I walk, Bob, Jill, and my atheist friends point, with similar conviction, to its absence. There's no middle ground.

It's a fatal, epistemological and otherwise, division.

Although I can accept this intellectually, I frequently shiver at its emotional implications. And complications. The movie "Come Sunday" presents the true story of a minister named Carlton Pearson. Pearson was a prominent preacher in the African American Pentecostal tradition, who was widely revered for his ability to bring an audience to its feet in praise of God. In addition to shepherding one of the largest churches in Tulsa, Oklahoma, Pearson spoke regularly at churches all over the country. Everyone, it seemed, wanted him.

One day, however, Pearson came to believe that, despite what he had been taught—and had taught—all of his life about the eternal destiny of those who do not believe in Jesus (which, according to the tradition in which he had been raised, is hell), he had been wrong. No, God will not condemn unbelievers to hell. Those who choose not to accept God in this life will not be punished in the next. All will be chosen, all will be saved.

Needless to say, Pearson's change of heart, a conclusion to which he came after many agonizing days and nights of thought, study, and prayer, did not sit well with many in his congregation. The elders and bishops of his tradition soon declared him to be a heretic. Pearson lost most of his congregants, had to sell off the church building and everything in it, and became, in the eyes of many within and outside of his tradition, *persona non grata*. He and his views were deigned anathema.

Many years later, after some painful and difficult transitions of body, spirit, and soul, Pearson now preaches at a Unitarian church in Tulsa. He's at peace.

In his book *Farewell to God,* author Charles Templeton, for many years a close associate of the evangelist Billy Graham, describes how after much soul searching, he decided to leave the evangelical world. He writes of how certain issues, among them the vexing problem of God and evil, prompted him to conclude that he could no longer, in good conscience, remain with Graham's organization. Templeton said "farewell" to God.[7]

My question is therefore this: if, as I firmly believe, Jesus is the only way to God, how do I deal with the conclusions of those who, though they once believed this as much as I do, decide to move in a different direction?

Particularly if there is no middle ground.

Some might of course argue that Pearson and Templeton succumbed to the wiles of Satan, that in their quest for understanding, they inadvertently opened themselves to the influences of the "dark" side. That they let their emotions get the better of them, that they confused faith with feeling. That they allowed themselves to get carried away by worldly philosophy and thought. While all of these things may well contain a measure of truth, what is troubling is that, as far as anyone can tell, at one time both men were *bona fide* evangelicals, as in love with Jesus as any other Christian. This means, in turn, that they possessed the "mind" of Christ (1 Corinthians 2:13), and that the Holy Spirit (per Paul's words in the eighth chapter of his letter to the church at Rome (Romans 8:26)) was constantly monitoring and

---

[7] It is perhaps worth noting that in an interview with author Lee Strobels when the latter was writing his *Case for Christ,* Templeton admitted that he still "missed" Jesus.

guiding their prayers to God. In theory, they ought not to have rejected their prior beliefs.

But they did. Moreover, it doesn't work to argue that both men never really believed in Jesus in the first place. That's offensive and arrogant.

If there is no middle ground, however, I'm left scrambling. Why must there even be a God? Or as a passage (Menahot 29) from the Talmud implies, sometimes even God cannot believe in God!

Some years ago, as I was grading papers during one of my prep periods, a student approached me and asked if we could talk. Sure. We left my classroom and went into the school's chapel. As we sat in the seats, together looking at the pulpit and stage, the banners on the walls, and the piano and organ, Ben shared what was on his mind and, it turned out, his heart. That past weekend, he, I, and a number of other students had camped for two nights in a local state park. We had a great time, hiking, talking, building fires, making s'mores, and appreciating the opportunity to leave our routines behind. As I always did when I led trips of this nature, I took a little time on Sunday morning, before we left the park, to share some words and thoughts from the Bible. Was anyone listening? It was difficult to tell; everyone's face was rather blank!

At least one person was listening, however: Ben. He told me that he had heard and seen something over the weekend, something he had not heard and seen before. He said that he had felt touched by God in a way he had never experienced or imagined.

At the core of what he was saying was Ben's sense that something was missing in his life, something that, until this weekend, he hadn't known he *had* been missing. For the first time, he felt a need, a deeply personal need for a richer relationship with his creator. Not that he didn't have human friends or a loving family; he absolutely did. Over and above these things, however, Ben had come to conclude that although he treasured these relationships, he needed another relationship, another relationship in which he believed these transient connections would find meaning. "I'm tired of being lonely," he said, "I'm tired of wondering whether I will always have friends. I want a permanent friend. I want to be friends with God."

We prayed. As I spoke, Ben repeated my words after me. "Lord Jesus," I said, "thank you for your love in our lives. Thank you that you love Ben. Thank you that you want to be our friend. 'Lord, I confess my sins, my decisions to wander from your love. I confess it all. I believe that Jesus died for my sins. I now believe it in my heart.'"

Ben told his mother about his decision when he got home that afternoon. She wept. She had waited many years for this day. Ben subsequently told his friends: they were uniformly thrilled. And he told his girlfriend. Jasmine, who had been a Christian since she was very young, could not contain her happiness. The story didn't end there. After several more years, Ben and Jasmine married and, to both their parents' immense joy, soon presented them with a grandchild (and a couple of years later, one more). All was, and remains, well.

I cannot definitively prove God is there. I cannot definitively understand *why* or *how* God is there. But I can, in faith, live in his effects.

It's an enduring conundrum.

When I set out to find a church to attend after I moved to East Texas, all I could see were Baptist churches. And more Baptist churches. There was a First Baptist, a Second Baptist, a Missionary Baptist, a Primitive Baptist, an Ebenezer Baptist, and a Calvary Baptist, to name just a few. In addition, there were a number of Baptist churches which had been named after the street on which they were established: Cherry Street Baptist, Long Street Baptist, East Main Street Baptist. It seemed endless. The aphorism which I had long heard about the South, "A church on every corner," suddenly became very real to me: it was more than true!

Because it was slightly out of town and its buildings looked less intimidating than the those of the lofty and ornate First or Second Baptist churches downtown, churches that the "landed gentry" of Henderson attended, I chose East Main Baptist. With a modest white steeple and a neat and tidy front lawn, it looked like a church in which I'd feel at home.

I was right. Although our cultural backgrounds could not have been more different—the former hippie revolutionary from California and the politically conservative rural Southerners—I found much to like in the church. Everyone welcomed me with open arms, happily integrating me into their congregational life. The pastor and his wife treated me as one of their children, and numerous members regularly invited me over for Sunday afternoon "dinner" after church services.

In addition to attending worship services, I attended Sunday school. While I had begun to study the Bible on my own and was coming to a modicum of understanding of what it was all about, I had yet to grasp its bigger pictures, much less the finer points of its doctrine. I soaked up talk of things like the unpardonable sin (blasphemy against the Holy Spirit (Matthew 12:31-32)); the exclusivity of Jesus ("I am the Way, the Truth, and the Life; no one comes to the Father but by Me" (John 14:6)); and the end of the world (one day, one day not too far away, my teacher said, Jesus will return and "take us all home" (1 Thessalonians 4:13-17)). It was all very interesting, and at times overwhelming: I had not yet developed any categories to process it.

After a time, I started attending the Sunday evening gathering, too. It was called Training Union. I also came on Wednesday night for choir practice: several congregants told me I had a good voice for it. In some ways, church was all I knew.

East Main Baptist was a church steeped in social formality. I rarely set foot in the sanctuary unless I was wearing a suit, and never did I dress in anything other than slacks and polo shirts. (Although I did wear shorts when one Sunday my car wouldn't start and I rode my bicycle to church, an activity which amused my fellow church members to no end.) Had I stepped away for a moment and looked at myself, I might well have wondered who I really had become. It was a far, far cry from the wild and wooly world of the American counterculture which I had inhabited up until a little over a year and a half before.

When I left Henderson to work at the Christian camp, away from the social strictures of the tiny town in which I had been living, however, I saw another side to the story. Released, as it were, from what now seemed to be cumbersome cultural expectations about dress and behavior,

I felt freer than I had in years. I realized that I had become old before my time. So determined had I been on investing myself in the new way of existence that I believed trusting Jesus had opened to me that I had come to believe as if I needed to discard completely all vestiges of the person I had been before. So fully did I push myself to do this that, I now realized, I had inadvertently suppressed, even eradicated who I was. I had lost my sense of humor, my sense of outdoor adventure, my interest in rock music, and much more.

I loved it: Christianity could actually be fun!

The kicker, however, is that I had to be "new" even as I was being "old." I had to believe even as I did not. Traditions do not die easily. And faith is often built upon them.

Many decades ago, well before I came to faith, I was traveling through the hinterlands of northern Minnesota, hitchhiking my way across its rolling landscapes of lake and field, my destination undefined, my heart entirely open to what I would find. Walking along a stream one night, sounds of bullfrogs ringing in my ear, stars sparkling overhead, I glanced to the south to see, silhouetted against the nearly full moon, a formation of Canada geese moving across the sky. How, I thought, can I possibly understand this? How can I ever begin to fathom what this wonder means? I felt so helpless, so abjectly helpless: I was so tiny, so small. The world was talking to me and I couldn't hear a thing.

Over forty-six years later, although I may understand more about myself and my life and, I like to think, God, I'm still helpless. I'll always be ignorant of the full movements of God. I'll always be standing before intention and activity I will never fully grasp or be able to change. I must ever trust what I can't see in what I can. It's vexing, it's frustrating. But faith cannot be any other way. Nascent and inchoate clarity must always outweigh the perspicuity of the present.

This is the exquisite, shall I call it, torture of faith. When I finished seminary and was casting about for my next move, the road looked very dark. The world didn't seem to need another humanities major, much less a seminarian. No one cared that I had a master's degree; no one cared that I could write well; no one cared that I had administrative skills. Dallas, the city to which I had moved after graduating to be closer to Carol; Dallas, the home of dozens of gargantuan Christian churches; Dallas, the headquarters of multiple parachurch organizations; Dallas, a city caught up in its love for the TV series "Dallas" and the Dallas Cowboys (whom many called "God's team"), had nothing for me.

All I could find was a janitorial position, and this only because one of my seminary classmates, a guy who had moved to the city a couple of years before to marry the woman of his dreams (I was best man at his wedding), had an opening. Otherwise, I could find nothing.

As I cast about for solutions to my angst, I came upon a book called *What Color is Your Parachute?* It's a perennial best seller about finding one's life vision. Perhaps you've read it. As I purchased a copy and began reading, one of the first questions I was asked to answer was this: what disappoints you the most?

Even before I finished reading the question, an answer popped into my head: God. Yes, God. The God to whom I had given my heart in the mountains of Jasper, Alberta, some six years before; the God whom I constantly credited with infusing my life with a purpose for which I had sought years and years; the God to whom I had striven to account nothing but good, yes: this God. It was this God, the God of love and compassion, the God of omniscience and power, the God of undying affection for his beloved, yes: this God. It was this God who was proving to be not only my greatest happiness, but also my greatest sorrow. Weeks and months and years of study, prayer, and waiting, weeks and months and years of looking for some direction, and nothing, absolutely nothing. Hours of anxiety, hours of exasperation, hours of wondering why I was even here, why I had even bothered going to seminary, why I had even bothered becoming a Christian. What was the point? Why had God given me new life only to dash me against a rock?

Or as Job put it, "Why is light given to a man whose way is hidden, and whom God has hedged in?" (Job 3:23)

Sure, I had read the stories of waiting. I had read how Abraham waited for a son; I had read how Moses had waited for his calling; I had read how Paul had waited to begin his ministry. And more. The Bible is filled with stories of people who wait. People who waited years, and then some, for God to deliver. People, to return to the eleventh chapter of Hebrews, who waited in vain.

A woman I knew in seminary, a woman who was probably ten years older than most of us, had for many years been looking for a husband. Well meaning people, mostly, unfortunately, men, spoke to her often about the virtue of waiting. "You must wait, Karen," they said, "you must wait. You must be patient. You must trust." As the old hymn goes, they added, you, Karen, must "Trust and obey, for there's no other way to be happy in Jesus, but to trust and obey."

Easy for them to say, I guess.

Sad to say, infused and excited about my newly obtained biblical knowledge, one night I contributed to Karen's turmoil, too, stolidly reminding her of how long various biblical figures (some of whom I mentioned above) waited for the fulfillment of what God had promised them. In typically ignorant male Christian fashion, I actually felt as if I was doing her a favor!

After all, did I not have the "knowledge"?

"Oh, I know how long people waited," she quickly replied, then added, as carefully as she could, "but this doesn't solve my problem. I'm still not married."

Fortunately, I didn't have the temerity or alternately, conceit, to suggest that maybe marriage was not God's will for her. At least I was sufficiently aware of my young believing self to realize that, in all candor, I couldn't know God's will for myself, much less for anyone else. Some years after I graduated, I heard from a friend of Karen's that she had indeed married. And that she was living happily "ever after."

Little did I know at the time, however, how long *I* would need to wait for various dreams of mine to find fulfillment. And in like manner, the many years it would take for me to reach a point where I had to admit that some of these dreams would *never* be fulfilled. Faith is a hard lesson. I trust and obey, yet I trust and obey in and amidst the impenetrability at the very heart of earthly existence. Although the presence and goodness of God illuminates this existence, it severely muddles it as well: a hint of ambiguity always remains.

And I never know how much there is.

Furthermore, as I continued to look around the wastelands, in my view, of Dallas, I saw countless other

Christians, Christians my age, who had fulfilling and well paying jobs, Christians to whom, it seemed, God had revealed some direction, some form of trajectory and blessing. People who seemed to know, in God, where they were going, and who were using their education for useful ends. Christians for whom God did not seem to be a disappointment.

I felt betrayed by God. I felt betrayed by the one who had delivered me from the clutches of spiritual aporia. In my darkest moments, I invoked Jesus' plaintive cry from the cross, "My God, my God; why have you forsaken me?" as emblematic of my present plight. I felt as if God had indeed abandoned me, as if he had stopped caring about what happened to me. It was very difficult, even more difficult, I'd say, than my most impoverished days as a seminary student, those days, which I mentioned earlier, of near financial insolvency. At least I knew where I was going the next day.

Now I did not.

Herein, however, is the paradox: I never stopped believing in God. As I have said several times, prayerful fulfillment is not faith's point. Once more: God is not a slot machine. He is a personal, holy, and loving being with whom I am in relationship. Hence, all things considered, I knew that I was better served to trust God than not. The rest is ancillary. Integral, yes; definitive, no.

It can be a very rough road. But it is meaningful.

Despite my angst, I continued to attend church each week, singing hymns like one that is based on Psalm 5, whose opening lines go, "Give ear oh Lord, my God, consider my meditations. Hearken unto the cry of heart, my king and my God." I tried to believe that God heard me, that he heard my longings, that he heard my pain and lament. In addition, although I occasionally felt as if my doing so was a perfunctory act, I continued to read my Bible every morning. I wanted to believe that even if God abandoned me, I could still hear him speak. At all costs, I clung to belief.

It seems irrational, doesn't it?

On the other hand, at this juncture in my Christian journey I had experienced too many things to dismiss my faith as irrationality. Some years before, when I lived in East Texas and before I started attending church there, I "backslid." For five months, without directly intending to yet without directly intending not to, I rejected the thoughts and community of God. When one day a friend of my sister Ellen called me from Houston to say that she was traveling through Texas and would I like to visit her this weekend, I quickly got on a bus going to that hot and humid metropolis some two hundred miles to my south. Carmen was staying with some friends in the western part of the city. We hung out that day, Carmen and I, talking and strolling through some of Houston's many neighborhoods, then returned to her friends' apartment for the night. The next morning, as I was getting ready to leave, I invited her to come to Henderson.

Two people alone in a big house (my roommates had left for the July 4th break), both somewhat lonely, both ready for a new adventure; spiritually speaking, it was not a healthy combination. I stumbled hard, plunging headlong into an intense sexual adventure, the lust of my heart blissfully eliding the discipline of my mind, as I summarily dismissed the value of everything I had been taught about Jesus.

For although I didn't know much, I knew enough

to understand that part of being a believer in Jesus was abstaining from sex before marriage. Barely four months after my conversion, shortly after I learned that I had a job in East Texas, I left my parents' home in Los Angeles (where I had been staying since I returned from my mountain forays in Canada) to travel across the country. The first stop I made was Springfield, Missouri, to visit Ken, a good friend from high school.

Like me, Ken had changed, dramatically. A couple of years before I found Jesus, he had done the same. No longer did he take drugs, no longer did he pursue sexual dalliance, no longer did he go wild and crazy playing the Who's "Magic Bus" every time I saw him. And he had unbearably short hair. With my hair still falling to my elbows, I was amazed at the extent of Ken's transformational shift. It seemed only yesterday that he and I had smoked a joint together.

Most astonishing was that Ken now attended a Bible college. And it was not just any Bible college. It was *Baptist* Bible College. Baptist Bible College was unlike anything I had experienced. The six day creation theory was paramount and evolution was the work of the Devil; daily chapel attendance was required; student attire was a tie and jacket for men and modest skirt and high neckline blouse for women; and chaperones mandated on first, second, and maybe third dates. I was amazed: how could such a place even exist?

But Baptist Bible College was a place of tremendous love. Thinking I was a "lost" soul, a wayward hippie who desperately needed Jesus or, to use their term, a person who needed "to be saved," everyone, professors on down, reached out to me. Once they realized that I in fact believed in

Jesus, however incomplete my understanding was of him at the time, they shifted from evangelism to discipleship. I learned so much.

Part of this was being taught that anyone who does not believe in Jesus during her life will, upon death, be consigned to a fiery hell, destined to burn forever and ever. The thought of this happening to members of my family led me, midway through my stay in Springfield, to write letters to each of them—Mom, Dad, Bob, Ellen, and Kathleen—warning them of the potential peril of dismissing Jesus. It took many months, even years, to undo the damage this did to our relationships.

Toward the end of the week, I walked into a barber shop and asked the barber, an older man named "Dude Fellows," to cut my hair. Stunned and thinking I was joking, he demurred. But after I and my new friends insisted to him that I was serious, he took up the task. Hair covered the floor of the tiny shop, tufts and strands of brown sprinkled everywhere.

The ethos of sexual restraint was driven into me most acutely my last night at the college (I stayed with Ken in his dorm room for a week). Ken came home from a date with his girlfriend Diane to say that he had asked her to marry him. Wow: marriage? It seemed unlike anything I might associate with Ken.

There was more. After recounting to me the story of how he asked her, Ken added, "We will not have sex until after the wedding. It's really important that we wait. It's what God wants."

Oh. At this point, given everything else I had been told that week and the respect that I had always had for Ken, I took his statement as gospel truth. Absolutely: no sex until marriage. Caught in the throes of passion with Carmen, however, I facilely set this instruction aside: did it really matter?

Oddly, it seemed that it did. After Carmen left, hitchhiking her way to the East Coast for more adventure, I, now eager for more physical debauchery, soon took up with another woman I knew from work. Things progressed. One weekend, we went camping in Arkansas's Ozark mountains. Although day and night, forest or stream, I went wild for her, I found myself pestered by a nagging thought that I was doing the wrong thing. How curious. Subsequently, everywhere I then traveled, be it on long bicycle rides into some of the most forgotten stretches of rural Texas, hiking around the lakes of southern Arkansas, or trekking through the chigger infested woods of western Louisiana, I encountered something that made me stop and think about what I was doing. Whether it was a poster advertising an evangelistic talk at a church, an interview in a newspaper, or a seemingly random encounter with a person who talked to me about Jesus, I could not seem to escape the "eye" of God. The harder I tried to move away from my spiritual birth, the more it seemed that God would not let me forget it. I began to feel how I felt before I came to belief when everywhere I went I bumped into someone who talked to me about Jesus. Of how I could not, no matter what I thought or did, it seemed, elude, as some have called it, the "hound of heaven."

Nor could I now. After a few weeks of convicting encounters, I concluded that, try as I might, I was foolish to ignore or undo the change that God had wrought in my soul. I left Jan, "returned" to God, and never looked back again.

Illogical coincidence or a logical God?

Granted, any number of people might say that I wasn't really hearing God in these various encounters with words and people from "church world," but only the confusion of an imaginary guilt. I was beating myself up over someone/something that had never existed to start with.

Maybe. On the other hand, in all my years of spiritual wandering, I never asked to believe in Jesus. Not once. It rather seems that he believed in me. That despite my constant and repeated rejections of him, he continued to pursue me. To wit, although I may find it easy enough to let go of something I didn't create, I find it nearly impossible to let go of something that has created *me*.

Sure, as I noted in my brief descriptions of the lives of Carlton Pearson and Charles Templeton, there are many people who, although they were "born again," have since wandered away, never to return to, as it were, God. Many, such as Matt Dellahunty, current president of the Atheist Community of Austin, Texas, have become aggressively militant atheists. I can't see the inner workings of these individuals' hearts; I cannot pretend to know everything that went into their decision. I can only explain myself.

It's complicated, this music that is always playing.

Perhaps if I had grown up believing, perhaps if I had been raised to accept Jesus at a very young age, perhaps if I had known nothing but Christianity, I might see this differently. Any spiritual rebirth that I might have experienced would have been so well woven into my childhood imagination that I would have had nothing with which to compare it. I would have had nothing to cause me to think otherwise.

Which is why, despite the many spiritually frustrating roads on which I traveled prior to my conversion, I remain thankful that I did not come to Jesus any earlier than I did. I am grateful that I have seen both sides. I am thankful that I can see, see clearly, the "me" who is the new creation.

Moreover, it's no secret that it is often the people who grow up in Christian homes who, if they stray, become the most hostile toward it. It's hard to imagine something you've not experienced; it's often easier to climb over the wall and never look back. Ask Siddhartha.

Nonetheless, I can name many, many people who have grown up in the faith and are leading lovely and fulfilling lives. Though they know full well, culturally speaking, what lies on the "other side," they decided long ago that it is not for them. They're in God to stay.

As, I realized, was I. To borrow a phrase from Job, "Though he [God] should slay me, I shall trust him" (Job 13:15). Not that God had been trying to slay me, but that, as I have recounted, he sometimes seemed to care very little for my problems, emotional, vocational, financial, or otherwise. He disappointed me frequently. Still does.

But I knew then, and I still know now, that I could not reject him. I knew that I had tried it once, and failed. I knew that, for better or worse, I should—and would—cling to God. I would continue to believe that of all things on this planet, the most important, by far, is the fact and presence of God. To piggyback on Martin Luther's words as he stood before his questioners at the Diet of Worms, "Here I stand, I can do no other."

The mystery, and challenge, of faith is that only God, in and of himself, makes, in this confusing and fractured reality, sense. It's a mystery because I can't believe otherwise; it's a challenge because as a human being I *can* believe otherwise.

Belief is an experience. And like any experience, it has its ups and downs. Yet it seems that the longer I continue in this experience, the more extreme each becomes. One moment, I shout my love for Jesus clearly; the next moment, I'm in utter despair over my sin.

So it must be. As the Indian writer and mystic Rabindranath Tagore once observed, it is only in sorrow and despair that the infinite manifests itself most fully.

A couple of months after I moved to Dallas, Carol and I were invited to serve as counselors at a Christian camp on Cape Cod. I quit my janitorial job, Carol took a leave of absence from her job, and together we drove halfway across the country to the tiny town of Sandwich, Massachusetts. All in all, we had a good summer. Because I directed the camp's "nature center" and did not therefore have a cabin of eight energetic boys with which to contend, however, I probably had a better time than Carol. She was assigned to supervise a cabin of spoiled and unruly teenage girls who had come to the camp very much aware that they were only there because their parents wanted a break from them. She did not get much sleep.

On our one day off each week, we traveled as far as we could from the camp. We usually went to Boston to enjoy its many sights and cultural opportunities. We left very early in the morning and did not return until the last possible time we were required to report back. Though we both grew spiritually, I suspect Carol did the most. Her daily struggles with her girls (along with her tireless efforts to help one of them who had cerebral palsy overcome her fear of the water and learn how to swim) knit the fact of God's presence ever more deeply into her heart. She knew it, she felt it.

On the other hand, I left Cape Cod feeling as about spiritually empty as I had been when I arrived. I still felt as if I was in a spiritual wilderness. Faith is an experience, yes, but so is God.

Upon our return, I had to look for another job. My prospects looked as dim as they had seemed the previous spring. Despite daily searching, I found nothing. One day, however, I got a call. I was to be a clerk, a Case Control Clerk, to use the official "federalese" language, for the South Central region of the Social Security Administration in Dallas. Was this God's answer to my prayers?

I guess. Yes, the income from this job enabled me to live, and yes, it allowed me to pay my bills. But it was not what I had gone to seminary for. It was an office job, pushing paper and bureaucratic nonsense. Although in an effort to inspire me, Dad often reminded me that Albert Einstein was a clerk at the time he announced what would become known as the Theory of Relativity, I hardly found it consolation. I spent my days roaming through reams of paper and telephone calls to help the office's fraud investigators ferret out people who were taking advantage of the laws governing the various disbursements that constitute Social Security. I could probably count on one hand the number of times I had fun.

As I had the previous spring, I wondered why. I wondered why I was here. And I had to ask myself, again, whether it was still God who disappointed me the most.

Could be. Although I tried to be diligent and do my best, to do my best for God, I nonetheless labored with a grief, an acidic grief that gnawed at my innermost being. I just didn't understand. But I thought often about the joy of my conversion moment; I thought frequently of the happiness of my recent engagement to Carol. I remembered my joy of mountains, I affirmed my delight in reading the Bible. What and where would I be without God? Sure, I might be happy, and sure, I might have found a beautiful relationship and satisfying employment. Nonetheless, I knew full well that I would still wonder, would still wonder as I had done almost every day of my "previous" life: is this all there is?

I would still wonder about eternity.

I often told myself, however, that even though I no longer wondered about eternity in this way, I had in fact, in a curious irony, replaced one wondering with another. Once, I had wrestled against God. And I lost. Now, I was wrestling with God. And I was still losing. Like Jacob on the River Jabbok (Genesis 32), I was, to put it rather crassly, damned if I do and damned if I don't. I knew, and still do, that for the rest of my earthly existence, I would struggle to reconcile God's presence with the ontological ruptures of this world.

My acknowledgement of God's fact and presence offers me a way into meaning. It also frequently prevents me from seeing any way out. As musician Nina Simone once put it, "I fight with God every day."

In an entirely good way. In August of 2011, my siblings and I met in Los Angeles to complete the sale of Mom and Dad's house. I arrived a couple of days before everyone else, so I had some alone time in the walls of my childhood home.

I appreciated the opportunity. I walked through the rooms for a couple of hours, carefully reflecting on the colossally poignant spans of event and time that each contained. On occasion, it was overwhelming. On Saturday of that week (I arrived on Thursday), sister Kathleen flew in from Santa Rosa for, as she put it, her "time." After picking her up at the airport, I dropped her off at the house, leaving her to her meditations. I set my sights for Claremont, a little city about sixty miles to the east. There, I knew, lived one of my best friends from college, Lynn, now married to Roy. I had not seen them in over fifteen years.

Though I did not have Lynn's phone number or email, I remembered her street address. I resolved to show up at their doorstep, sight unseen. Why not?

It didn't matter. Lynn and Roy were delighted to see me. And vice versa. We had a fun day. After we talked a while in their living room, Roy and I bicycled to a nearby park, a park he visited often. Along the way, I, ever the inquisitive theology student, asked Roy about his religious background. He told me that he had grown up in a conservative fundamentalist church. "Were you saved?" I asked him.

"Yeah, when I was eight years old. I walked to the front of the church and gave my heart to Jesus."

Roy had heard the music once. Now he didn't seem to hear it at all: he hadn't been in a church in decades. Nor did he ever read the Bible.

When we returned from our ride, Roy showered and left to attend to some business. Lynn and I walked into town. Mom's passing still very much on my mind, I kept thinking of the third chapter of Ecclesiastes' observation that, "There is a time to give birth, and there is a time to die." I had read this verse every morning the week before she died. I therefore wondered as I spent that day with Lynn whether death was nothing more than our given destiny, that whether, God or not, Mom's passing was simply an expression of the natural rhythms of existence. Painful, yes, but biologically speaking, quite normal.

And questions no longer matter.

After lunch, Lynn mentioned that she didn't think she believed in God. No surprises there. Although she had been raised Jewish in upstate New York, by the time she came to college, Lynn had essentially abandoned any semblance of loyalty to its theological presuppositions.

There was not much I could say: we had both traveled many miles since college.

But I did think about a long ago winter night, a night only a couple of months before our graduation when, on my home from a party, I paused to stand on the edge of the fields that surrounded our student apartment complex. Snow was falling, stars were beaming. Coated with fresh whiteness, the tangles of dry grass, pushing into the light of the half moon, shone with a brumal sparkle. Lovely, lovely, I thought.

I wondered what it all meant.

I heard some crunching on the path. I turned: it was Lynn. She and I stood together for some time, jointly bewitched by the flakes drifting through the night. "I'm gonna sleep out there tonight," I said.

"I know," she said, "it's in you."

"Yeah," I replied, "it's me."

So I believed. The following fall, when I found myself in Jasper, resting a sore ankle tendon midway through my four month trek through the Canadian Rockies, I received a letter from Lynn. It was a poem. "He wants to talk," it began, referring to my oft expressed frustrations with my stuttering in my final year of college, "and he thinks he can't. But he talks more than anyone else I know. He talks like the mountains, the mountains he loves. The mountains are in him."

When I looked up from the page, I felt as if Lynn and I were looking directly into each other's eyes. She knew me. She knew that, for me, it was mountains that constituted the sum of all that was possible, all that was real, all that was there. What more could I in any way need?

More than I could imagine, it seemed. Four years after that day in Jasper, I started my third year of seminary. I soon realized that Lynn and I were only living about twenty miles from each other. We should get together!

During one visit, I shared with Lynn a prayer letter that I sent to some friends and supporters each month. After reading it, she asked me, "Billy, do you believe that people shouldn't have sex before they are married?"

Memories of East Texas "deviancy" popped into my head. "Yes," I said.

"Oh, Billy!" she exclaimed, "how could you?"

I felt queasy: the abyss between faith and unbelief had never seemed so insuperably stark. I had certainly traveled many, many moons, chronologically, figuratively, and theologically, since that winter night outside Green Bay. And though I still had the note she wrote me in Jasper, I knew its day was now long, long past.

How does one reconcile transcendent conviction, a conviction of faith without sight, with such a compelling, and very much present, human desire? I didn't know where, really, to begin.

On this lovely autumn day in Claremont, however, all that was behind us. Lynn was less dogmatic; I was more willing to listen. Yet as I heard Lynn recount the rhythms of her life, and I mine, I could not help returning to that verse from Ecclesiastes three. Apart from a cohering framework, a final integrating point, life really was futile. It's grand, indeed, but absent a teleology of greater purpose, it is no more than a series of events, sometimes connected, sometimes not, a train of happenstances driven by our burning urge to live. Although we love and treasure our lives and will do almost anything to extend and preserve them, we will always live in the shadow of that observation: "There is a time to die." Then what?

"Life is futile," I said to Lynn.

"But we can still live it to the fullest."

True enough, but I felt as if we still had not resolved the nagging issue: what, in the big picture, has been the point?

Or as Spruce said to me as he, Linda, and I sat by a lake one afternoon midway through our backpack in the San Juan Range of the Rockies a couple of years ago, "Life's not futile. But it ends."

Yes. Fresh cup of tea in hand, I had been meditating, for the umpteenth time, on a verse in the ninth chapter of Ecclesiastes. It reads, "This is an evil in all that is done under the sun, that there is one fate for all humans. Furthermore, the hearts of humans are full of madness and vexation is in their hearts throughout their lives. Afterwards they go to the dead."

It's a peculiar mix. Though we can find meaning even

in madness and aggravation, we are still doing so under the aegis of life's finality. Even the most inscrutable existential puzzles will one day come to an end.

And they never return.

At the time of our backpack, Spruce was only a few months from the passing of his mother. Watching her die had kindled a new interest in the supernatural in him. "There must be something bigger out there," he often said as we hiked, "but I have no idea what it is."

Even, I thought, in futility. But then it wouldn't be futile. We cannot ponder the mysterious and unknown without finitude, yet we cannot have, if life is to mean anything, finitude without any mystery.

We're terribly human.

The paradox is acute: if we love life and reject God, we confront futility. Yet if we love life and accept God, we confront frustration. Either way, we face the fact of ourselves.

With no way out. Except, as John remarks in his first letter, by faith, the faith that he calls "the victory that overcomes the world" (1 John 5:5).

I've been praying for Spruce for over forty years. I want him to hear the music.

On the other hand, maybe, I thought as I drove back to Los Angeles after my day with Lynn and Roy, there is no futility. There is no puzzle, there is no secret. Maybe life's brevity is simply a mirror of the inevitabilities implicit in this existence. Life's not futile; it's just life.

And life, as my friends at the Ayn Rand Institute remind me constantly, is the "highest value." We live it as it is meant to be lived: as life itself. The world? Well, to quote my friends again, "It just is." We need not ask why it is; we need only enjoy that it "is."

Fair enough. As I met the traffic of a Saturday afternoon in West Los Angeles, however, I still wondered whether this really answered the question. Or maybe there isn't a question to be asked.

Maybe. As I drove off the Santa Monica Freeway onto the 405, the San Diego Freeway, headed to the exit for Mom's house, however, I knew that I couldn't live with this sort of unanswerable question, this bedeviling ambiguity about existence. I needed more than my inner congratulations that the world "just is," and that I am "just here" to live meaningfully in it. Yes, wicked or righteous, famous or not, we can all enjoy life. And yes, whoever we are, we will all pass away. We have no choice. Moreover, once we are gone, no one will remember us. Indeed, given enough years, unless we were extraordinarily well known, we will vanish completely.

It's so Sisyphean.

For many years I've enjoyed clothing from the company Patagonia. Though its offerings can be pricey, they last indefinitely. Not too long ago, I picked its latest catalog out of our mail to see that it was dedicated to Jennifer Ridgeway. Patagonia's long time art director, Jennifer was responsible for some of the most iconic photos in the company's catalogs. Her husband Rick had, in his younger years, climbed K-2, without using artificial oxygen, and hiked across Borneo, sight unseen. Now he served as Patagonia's director of global outreach. In recent years, their children grown and their futures relatively secure, Rick and Jennifer had been looking to spend several more decades together adventuring around the globe.

Sadly, shortly before her seventieth birthday, Jennifer succumbed to cancer. I felt so sad. So young, so very young. It reminded me of the story of Doug Tompkins, founder of the mountaineering equipment company The North Face and, later, the clothing company Espirit. Doug was a very successful businessman. With the money he made from selling both companies, Doug and his wife Kris, once Patagonia's CEO, moved to Argentina. There they proceeded to use their money to buy up all the land they could so as to put together a series of national parks for the country. It was a laudable cause.

One day, Doug and some friends, including Yvon Chouinard, Patagonia's founder, went kayaking in one of the wildly remote rivers of the Patagonia region in South America. A storm soon came up, sending high, blustery winds across the water. Doug's kayak overturned, and he spent many minutes in the frigid blueness of the river. Too many. He died of hypothermia as he was being airlifted to a hospital. Doug was seventy-two. Wow, I had thought, wow: did he have any idea it would be his "time"? I recalled reading how in 1968 he, Yvon, and two others drove the length of the North American continent to scale, on Christmas Day, Fitz Roy, one of the most iconic peaks in Patagonia. The climbing world was amazed.

Doug had some remarkable adventures. He indeed lived life to the fullest. And now he was dead. I shivered at the disparity. Particularly if life "just is."

On her sixty-fifth birthday, I texted Lynn to send her my best wishes. She was very happy. And I was happy for her. Nonetheless, I grappled with the facts beneath the surface: one day it will all end. It will all end with nary a reason other than it had to be.

"I've got the joy, joy, joy, joy down in my heart, down in my heart. I've got the joy, joy, joy, joy down in my heart to stay. And I'm so happy, so very happy, I have the love of Jesus in my heart. I'm so happy, I'm just so happy, I have the love of Jesus in my heart."

We sang this song constantly at the camp in East Texas where, as I mentioned earlier, I served a summer as a counselor. Our day always began with a gathering of the entire camp population in the camp's assembly hall. Led by an enthusiastic leader, a woman whose persona bubbled with energy, we sang this song—and many others like it—for twenty minutes, revving up the campers for another fun day. As if they needed it. All of us felt happy; all of us were delighted to be singing together. We did indeed feel a joy down in our hearts.

Over forty years later, however, I wonder about this joy: what is it, really? And is it sufficient to counteract the certainty of death? Can we rejoice in simply being loved?

It seems we can: millions of us enjoy being loved. For most of us, being loved brings us immense happiness. But we all still die.

A number of years ago, as a member of a small group (many churches establish a network of groups of six to eight people to enable members to fellowship with each other at times other than Sunday morning) in the church we were attending in the early 2000's, I was asked to teach. I was happy and pleased to do it: aside from backpacking and exploring wild places, teaching is probably my favorite thing to do. Heidi, the de facto leader of the group, suggested Paul's letter to the church at Philippi. She wanted us to learn more about joy, a prominent motif in this letter.

My task therefore became deciphering, as best I could, what joy, in the Christian "life," means. Not that I had not thought about joy before, but this would be the first time I would do so for a specific teaching setting. As I researched and pondered, I thought back to the joy I experienced upon embracing Jesus' offer of abundant life. I remembered how I had felt overwhelmed with thankfulness and contentment. I remembered how my heart had burst with astonishment. I then looked back at my early years in the faith, the years in which regardless of what was happening in my life, I felt joyful and thankful. Nothing fazed me, nothing detracted: it was all good.

And I considered times since those days, times in which, particularly during worship, I felt a profound happiness, an abiding happiness of insight, enveloping, and purpose. Or when I had been backpacking and had come upon a new vista of mountain, lake, or meadow, a vista in which I had felt as if all who God is was shouting at me, filling me with gratitude and wonder. Or the innumerable times I had delighted when my children, particularly when they were toddlers, discovered something new about the world, a discovery in which they seemed more human than they had ever been before. Or happy moments with Carol, my siblings, and good friends. And many, many more instances of delight.

I also remembered the many times of downturn, some of which I have mentioned. I remembered how I didn't necessarily feel joyful, how I didn't necessarily felt content.

I remembered how I had struggled to believe, how I had wrestled, wrestled mightily to set my circumstances into a larger frame of hope. How I had cried, how I had wept. How I had called out to God in sorrow and frustration, wondering when this agony would end.

And how God didn't seem to respond. How he didn't seem to care. How he seemed so disappointing.

As Paul presents it in this letter, joy is not something I can quantify or put into a box. It is a condition of heart, a state of mind, an enduring, dare I say, permanent, state of inner contentment. It's a contentment of knowing that, over and above all else, God is there and that he is there in love. Joy is the ubiquity of God's presence: the fact and face of God. It is believing that because God is always there, loving, guiding, and working, always for the good of the world and everyone in it, we can relax. We can let go. We can be content. We can be joyful.

As the psalmist, "channeling" God in Psalm 46:10, urges us, "Relax, let go, be still, and know that I am God."

But it's complicated. Was Jesus joyful as he hung on the cross? He was. But Jesus was not joyful because of his circumstances. He was joyful because even in his darkest hour he believed he belonged to God. His was a joy that transcended all things, transcended even what, at this juncture, he had become—a son rejected by his father—because his joy was not secondary to his life or faith. It was its bedrock and expression.

When the letter of James urges its readers to "count it all joy" in times of trial (James 1:2), or when Paul writes, as I shared earlier, to "give thanks in all things" (1 Thessalonians 5:18), they are therefore not telling people to admit that life's darknesses make them happy. Nor are they encouraging people to put a bright and cheery face on everything that happens. Not at all. The things that happen to people, the many tragic things that occur regularly in the human experience, are, by any reasonable definition, decidedly not joyous. They are immensely sorrowful.

James and Paul are rather saying that if we set joy in the person of God, if we root the fact of our joy in the absolute presence of God, we can rejoice. Happy or sad, we assert and proclaim that God is there and this God is love. Joy does not hinge on our human ability to master or measure the pain in our material experience. To borrow a term from philosopher Alvin Plantinga, joy is most deeply grounded in the "properly basic" presence of God.

A presence, however, we can only believe. When our friend Mary Jane learned that her husband Al had collapsed and died from a heart attack, she had joy. Not joy in what had happened, but joy in the fact of God. I was crushed, absolutely crushed, when Dad died. But I had joy: God was there. We were aghast when we learned that Megan had cancer. Yet we knew God was there: our joy remained.

Why? Faith's joy places the onus for a way through tragedy on a trust in a factuality which, though it cannot readily prove it, believes its presence. It makes the visible affirm the invisible and the invisible the visible. It insists that although God is a God of this world, he is also a God of the world in which this world is contained. The paradox is excruciating. In a material world, the joy of faith avers that someone who is not material can explain what materiality cannot.

I quote a portion of Psalm 139:

> "For You [God] formed my inward parts; You wove me in my mother's womb. I will give thanks to You, for I am fearfully and wonderfully made; wonderful are Your works, and my soul knows it very well. My frame was not hidden from You when I was made in secret, and skillfully wrought in the depths of the earth; Your eyes have seen my unformed substance; and in Your book were all written the days that were ordained for me, when as yet there was not one of them." (Psalm 139:13-16).

If God has "woven" (rendered, in the original Hebrew, "knit together") us together, we could not be any other way than what we are. Nor should we ever think that we should be. Whatever flaws we therefore think we have are in fact not flaws in God's eyes but rather things that God will use to our—and his—greater good. They are not mistakes, and they are not errors. As God told Paul in a passage I cited earlier, God's grace is "sufficient" for who we are.

Really? On the one hand, as any psychologist will tell us, from every emotional standpoint, be it shaped by spiritual conviction or not, this makes perfect sense. We do ourselves no favors when we spend our lives regretting that with which we were born. We had no choice in who our parents were, and we had no choice in determining how the particular combination of genes that formed us worked out. All we can do is live with what we are given.

And above all else, strive to be content. To do otherwise is to invite perpetual unhappiness and emotional disaster. We will lose everything.

Even if, as American writer Joan Didion observed in a frequently cited quote, we tell ourselves "stories" to do so.

But what do we do if we are born severely disabled? Congenitally deformed? Chemically prone to depression? Summoning joy in God's goodness becomes significantly more difficult. Furthermore, saying to anyone, an unbeliever in particular, that in God's eyes we could not be any other than what we are, can, in some instances, stretch someone's skepticism to the breaking point. It does not seem logical.

From almost earthly standpoint, it's not. Yet to return to something I said earlier, faith will not necessarily make temporal sense. In fact, it will probably *never* make temporal sense. But it will make eternal sense. And it does so because God, and only God, makes eternal sense.

Yet this makes it all the more difficult. It asks you, it asks me, to ascribe joy to one and only thing: the fact and presence of an unseen God.

Again: really? A few summers ago, after attending a conference at Yale University on, ironically enough, joy and the good life, I took some time to visit some beloved college friends who lived on the East Coast. Two lived in Harford, Connecticut, not far from New Haven, where Yale is situated; the other in Gloucester, Massachusetts, about two and a half hours away. Mary and Hank live in central Hartford, where they raised their two children, both of whom are now living in New York City. Mary and Hank appreciate this, as it allows easy passage to see their growing brood of grandchildren. It's a couple of hours by train. Now that Mary is retired, she can see her grandchildren whenever her kids will have her. Hank is still working, happily, and doesn't get out as often. As he puts it, very much tongue in cheek, he must keep working, "In order to accommodate Mary in the lifestyle to which she has been accustomed."

Mary and Hank appeared to be very happy and content with their lives. When they were raising their children, they regularly attended a Unitarian church in town; now they only attend it occasionally. They believe strongly in the Unitarian ethos of tolerance and acceptance of all faith perspectives, and that, all things considered, people should be able to find some measure of common ground in terms of spirituality and the human exchange with the divine.

I cannot disagree. Knowing that I would be visiting Mary and Hank at the end of the summer, I had earlier picked up a copy of my *Imagining Eternity* to give to Mary. When I had last seen her, she expressed an interest in reading it. The morning I left, after Hank had gone to his law office, Mary and I took a walk through the parklands near their house. We talked. We talked of the ordinary and mundane, we talked of the deeper and beyond. What has made us happy? What has made us sad? What do we want to do with the rest of our lives?

Neither of us had any ready answers, only that we had had some wonderful times along the way. Overall, we had no reason to look back. We had been through our years; we had walked the paths before us. And now we were on the other side, well aware that the paths to come will be fewer than the ones that preceded them.

It was joyful and sobering.

As we chatted, I realized that, again, outside of affirming

what I believed to be the fact of a transcendent presence, I could do little else but agree with Mary: we live, we love, we die. It's glorious, it's depressing. It's life.

So, I thought, is my joy any greater than Mary's? Is my hope bigger than hers? Materially speaking, absolutely not. Absent a supernatural grounding for it, however, joy is no more than the evanescent fruit of an evanescent existence. Although I do not dispute that that some people are more joyful or hopeful than others (as Aunt Patty once told me, "They have the 'happy' gene"), in the biggest possible material picture these are simply measures on a continuum, the vast continuum of the possibilities of a material world. A world that will one day end.

So much did I therefore want to mention the idea of a transcendent presence. So much did I want to assert the notion of a personal God. So much did I wish to talk about the concept of eternity. But I didn't. Mary had my book; she had my love. I had to hope that the way in which I communicated my hope and joy of faith would resonate with her, and that she would come to see that although the joy of this life is indisputably grand, it is in the end merely a measure of the emotional plasticity of a material world.

I wanted so much for her to hear the music. But I knew that she might not. The thought made my heart ache with sorrow and longing. Once more, I encountered the galling impasse of faith: the options are so frightfully stark. And eons apart.

I was therefore feeling particularly poignant as I left Hartford, found I-95, and continued on to the Boston area. Poignant because I didn't know when I would see Mary and Hank again, poignant because there was always more to say than there is time to say it, and poignant because all of us, my dearest college friends and I, are living out our lives even as we know full well that life will one day, maybe one day very soon, pass us by.

It's heartbreaking. Yet so deeply human.

In contrast with the inner city environs of Mary and Hank, David and Margaret live in a beautifully renovated home perched on a peninsula overlooking the Atlantic. As they put it, they are "lucky." For many years, they had dreamed of living where they are living and when a few years ago they heard that a house had come up for sale on the peninsula, they immediately bought it: they knew exactly where the property was.

Being at that time professors at the University of Massachusetts, both David and Margaret had, like most academics, their summers off. We had plenty of time to talk. I soon detected a funny coincidence. As I mentioned, the topic of the conference I had attended was the theology of joy and the future of the good life. Margaret had just finished reading the *Book of Joy*, a lovely recounting of a conversation between the Dalai Lama and Archbishop Desmond Tutu about joy. Tutu, who counted the Dalai Lama among his good friends, had traveled to Dharmsala to help his friend celebrate his eightieth birthday. As they visited, the complier of the book, Douglas Abrams, asked questions and recorded their responses and observations. Like flies on the proverbial wall, we get a fascinating look at how two aging and deeply spiritually inclined men deal with the existential imperative that all of us face, the need to find meaning and joy and hope in an often meaningless and hopeless world.

As we kayaked that afternoon in the small bay on which their house sits, David and I rambled through a range of topics, from my hip surgery and recent job loss to my children to my backpacking, to his and Margaret's work to their time visiting a nephew in California and David's marvel at the waves of the Pacific, his choice of novels, his Quaker upbringing. It was at the end of the latter that David remarked that, "If I were to be anything, I guess I'd be a Quaker."

I was amused and, over dinner in their lovely patio area, told him so. "I'm not sure what you mean by 'anything,' but it seems that you're saying is that you're really not sure where you would like to land."

He smiled and nodded. Inwardly, though, I cringed: if I had not heard the music, I would not have cared one whit about whether David was inclined toward Quakerism or not. But I had. And that made it all the more heartrending. At one point during our meal, I asked David and Margaret whether, in their careers as epidemiologists, they had accomplished what they had set out to do. Both responded that they weren't sure what they had hoped to accomplish! But they were grateful to be doing what they were doing.

"What about you, Billy?'

"I didn't start out to be a teacher," I said. "Until I came to believe in Jesus, I really hadn't thought about it. But that moment changed everything."

The question that I surmised might now be in their minds was, how? How could one shift of belief change everything? After all, nineteenth century anarchist William Morris said the same thing about his "conversion" to the virtues of no government. He never looked back. And upon discovering Athabasca Pass while hiking through the Canadian Rockies, David Thompson, one of the most famous mountain men of the nineteenth century, wrote in his journal that he felt as if "a new world was before" him. It was a moment he never forgot.

My moment, however, was one driven by a belief that, beyond its emotional baggage, does not find its ground in this material world. It is a belief born of a conviction in the worth of things unseen, things which, despite the extent to which my experience, emotional and intellectual and cultural, testifies to their factuality, can nonetheless only be fully accessed and understood through faith.

Faith will always and ever be a hinge in a temporal world, a boundary between natural and supernatural. It's a presence, it's a promise, it's a prelude. It's not yet full. Faith is a key to a door whose opening will always be, in this life, a sightless shot across a finite world. The deepest import of its moment will always be elusive.

However, although this makes sense to me, it does not necessarily do so to anyone on this side of the door. That's the frustration. When I got home, I sent David and Margaret copies of a number of sermons and messages I had delivered over the years, a few chapters from books I had written, and an article on the meaning of the wilderness experience. My sermons and messages had to do with light, love, abandonment, pain, challenge and, most of all, joy. The book chapters dealt with hope and humility, the article with wisdom and loss.

In their responses to what turned out to be a fair number of pages of material, David and Margaret made several observations. Most interesting was one of David's.

He said that although he didn't understand everything I said (which, given that he had not to any extent inhabited the world of Christian theology and the esoteric language that too often accompanies it, was quite understandable!) he noted that I had achieved a joy which had sustained me, in great measure, throughout my life. You've "found" your joy, he said.

I was deeply moved. And not just because I was happy that someone had noticed, or that the influence of my belief systems may have showed. I was moved because without directly trying, I had managed to communicate that the joy of belief in God cannot be quantified or measured, emotionally, intellectually, or otherwise. It can only be experienced.

And it can only be experienced in faith. That's its wonder; it's also its aggravation. It all comes down to our willingness to affirm, in faith, the fact of God. To affirm the silent, loving, and superintending specter of the unseen and eternal God.

I realize that we have traveled many pages since my mention of the bible study on Philippians and my explanation of joy as an expression of enduring contentment in the fact of God's working presence. We've traveled even more pages since my sharing about the bible study I led in Ecclesiastes and my observation that, as a book, Ecclesiastes celebrates, in a profoundly paradoxical way, futility *and* joy, concluding that both are essential to humanness. How although we recognize the futility of finitude, we also acknowledge God's undergirding and enduring presence.

And how in the end, we put all these thoughts together.

We put all these together with our faith in God's eternal love.

If we want to.

One of the most famous psalms ever penned is Psalm 23. Often called the psalm of the Good Shepherd, Psalm 23 contains some of the most memorable lines in the Bible. "The Lord is my shepherd," it begins, "he makes me lie down in green pastures and leads me beside waters of rest." Therefore, "even though I walk through the valley of deep darkness, I fear no harm [evil], for You [Lord] are with me."

I rarely read the last verse without thinking of a sign that hung in a bedroom of a house in Victoria, British Columbia, where I stayed for several weeks in November of 1974. Offering its own, somewhat bemusing translation of this verse, this sign said, "Though I walk through the valley of darkness, I will fear no evil, for I am the meanest son of a bitch in the valley." The house belonged to Arthur, Dad's best friend who, after working in Los Angeles County for many years, took his retirement in Canada. There he lived with his wife and two sons, one around my age, the other two years older. Arthur spent much of his time doing wood carving, creating any number of sculptures to sell to the tourists who frequented the area. Everyone in the family became Canadian citizens.

Sadly, about ten years after my stay, Arthur's wife, Rae, developed lung cancer and, all too quickly, perished. She had not even retired. Eight years later, Joe, the older son, hanged himself and, some years after that, Ted, the younger one, died of alcoholism. Arthur himself died over twenty years ago. It all seemed so supremely tragic, a frightening testimony to the human freedom that, it seems we cannot live with but, ironically, we cannot live without, either.

I shiver to think about them today. Particularly as I recall some words emblazoned on the side of the Salvation Army building on downtown Victoria, "Jesus Christ is the same, yesterday, today, and forever" (Hebrews 13:8). Or when I remember the way that, before eating the lunch our East Texas community action agency provided for them each day, the gathered elderly prayed the Lord's prayer. Although they spoke most of the prayer softly, as they recited the final words, "For thine is the kingdom, the power, and the glory, forever," they were virtually shouting with conviction.

Or when I think about the frontispiece of my first Bible, a paperback New American Standard Version, which said, "The grass withers, the flowers fade; but the word of the Lord stands forever" (Isaiah 40:8).

I'll spend the rest of my days trying to reconcile God's longing for us and our pursuit of what he is not. And I will never fully understand the relationship of time and eternity. Nonetheless, I believe in both.

When I came upon the sign in the spare bedroom of Arthur and Rae's home, I was only a month removed from my turn to faith in Jesus, still trying to put it all together. I was also trying to balance my still very powerful memory of encountering a Jesus unleashed with my catechetical memories of seeing Jesus as a white man with blue eyes tending perfectly white sheep on a verdant set of Galilean hills. I had never much thought about what a valley of darkness might in fact mean.

Roughly five years before this time in Victoria, in fact, the first summer I backpacked, I solo hiked the 210 mile John Muir Trail, the iconic path that winds along the crest of California's Sierra Nevada mountain range (the range in which, I noted, I have so many good memories of camping with my family growing up). One day I came upon a particularly lovely meadow in a portion of the Range called Evolution Valley. Although I had seen innumerable meadows to this point, when I looked at this meadow (Colby Meadow by name) I was especially awestruck. Deeply green and covered with all kinds of wildflowers, Colby Meadow seemed to glide across the valley, its grasses flowing like an ocean tide from one side of the valley to the other, glistening in the afternoon sun. A stream ran lazily through it, dancing to the day, and a tree, a huge Lodgepole Pine, hovered on its bank, its needles tingling in the breezes gently sweeping over the yellow tussocks of the expanse. I wanted to leave the trail, hike to the tree, set up camp, and stay forever. I would spend my days touching the stream, the soothing stream that I felt was speaking to me of ultimate surcease and final rest. If hadn't known any better, I would have called it love.

I earlier shared a bit of my backpack, only few years from my conversion, through Colorado's Rocky Mountain National Park. On my third afternoon, I found myself at a picturesque set of lakes on the west side of the Continental Divide. As I set up camp, a woman approached. Her name was Sue and, I soon learned, she had recently come to believe in Jesus, too. After talking well into the night, we agreed to hike together the next day.

Sue worked, she said, at Celestial Seasonings, just down the road from the Park, in Boulder. Not too many other people believe in Jesus there, she said, but she was happy for the opportunity and the income it provided.

Not having been, at that point, much of a tea drinker, I was not terribly familiar with Celestial Seasonings. When I later looked it up, however, I liked what I saw. The company's specialty at that time was soft, soothing herbal teas, teas with amusingly quirky names like Candy Cane Lane, Country Peach Passion, Cranberry Apple Zinger, and Caramel Apple Dream.

It was a hippie's paradise!

As we climbed out of the lake basin, ambled over a few gentle ridges of tundra to reach the divide, and then began hiking back down to the trailhead from which I began, we stopped at a creek. It was a tiny creek, making barely a sound as it meandered through a meadow on the slopes of Mummy Mountain. Softly, ever so softly it watered the purple lupines and blue spruce trees clinging to its edges. Its waters shimmered in the afternoon sun. As I lay down in the cushioning grass and closed my eyes, I remembered Colby Meadow and Psalm 23. Waters of peace, waters of rest.

Yet I couldn't help but wonder whether other people, people who may not believe in Jesus, feel these waters of rest. Can we be free of God and still find them?

I should think so. Be it listening to music, watching a good play, seeing a memorable movie, doing meditation, or any number of other things, humans can experience the fullness of inner calm without turning to the idea of an omnipotent being who is overseeing all that is. They can find peace without God.

That, I guess, is the crux: faith in peace or the peace of faith? In a material world, a world in which peace comes in many shapes and forms, it's sometimes hard to tell. Knit with present transcendence, however, it's clearer: we're all loved by God.

But we all die.

Over ten years ago, Payson and I set out on a seven night expedition to climb to the summit of Mt. Whitney which, at 14,495 feet, is the highest peak in the contiguous U.S. Entering the Sierra on its east side, we took three days to hike the twenty-eight miles to the base camp for the ascent. We spent a day actually getting to the top, a sixteen mile round trip, then three days hiking back out. By the end of our first day of hiking out of Owens Valley, our starting point, we were feeling pretty good. We knew that aside from summiting Whitney, the most difficult part, an arduous ten mile hike out of the desert where we began, was over. From this point we would be on relative cruise control as we steadily ascended to our base camp. We would face no real obstacles in terms of slope or elevation.

The afternoon of our second day, we camped by a stream, Tyndale Creek, which ran along the border of a broad expanse of rich, green tundra that crawled across a lake basin on the western side of the Sierra crest. After we set up our tent, I grabbed a water bottle and walked to the stream. Removing my hiking boots and socks after the day of hiking, I dangled my feet in the cold waters, basking in the gentle alpine sun. How wonderfully perfect, I thought, how marvelously complete: what more, at this point, could I need?

I think often about these three experiences, Colby Meadow, Mummy Mountain, and Tyndale Creek, these experiences of waters of rest. I think about how I discovered these waters when I was far from God, about how I encountered them when I had only recently found God, and about how I enjoyed them many decades into walking with God. I still wonder how these experiences of rest come together. They are rests of human freedom, they are rests of divine favor. They are rests of ignoring the fact of God, they are rests of accepting the fact of God. Or both: I'm constantly juggling human freedom with divine presence.

Then there's love. Towards the close of his *Divine Comedy (Commedia),* Dante writes about the beatific vision, his experience of standing, in heaven (*Paradiso*) before God. I saw, he says, the "love which moves the sun and other stars." As Dante would have it, God's love orchestrates the movements of the cosmos and sustains the rhythms of the universe: it is that on which everything depends. God's love is ubiquitous and pervasive; it fills every point of existence. There is nowhere where God's love is not. There is nothing that is outside of it, there is nothing that escapes or eludes it. God's love suffuses, shapes, and guides all.

So does, if you recall, Paul say in the eighth chapter of his letter to the church at Rome. God's love will not leave us. Nor can we leave it, either.

I met Mike through the atheist discussion group. We've known each other for about nine years. Mike's wife, Jill, to whom he has been married nearly thirty years, is a born again evangelical Christian. Mike is an atheist for two reasons. One, as he puts it, is "the suffering of innocents." How could a good God allow such pain to be visited upon the most vulnerable of the world? Two, again, as he puts it, "God has not given us enough evidence of his existence. Why can't everyone have a 'road to Damascus' [a reference to the apostle Paul's life changing encounter with Jesus, recorded in Acts 9, as he traveled from Jerusalem to Damascus to identify more Christians to persecute] experience? If God is there, everyone should be having these kinds of experiences of him."

These arguments aside, what intrigues me about Mike is that he is living with evidence of faith and trust in God's love right in his home—his wife—and yet continues to insist that, as far as the universe is concerned, "There is no meaning." Surely, even the most skeptical researcher would admit that Mike's wife's affections for Jesus—and him— indicate that *someone* can find meaning in God in the midst of this cold, dark universe.

Even without "visible" evidence.

Mike also meets with his wife's pastor once a month for coffee and conversation. He and Scott talk widely about the truth claims of Christianity. But Mike remains unconvinced.

God's love may be real, but unless we believe it to be so, we will not see it.

Steve is one of my oldest friends. We've known each other since our sophomore days in college, when I arrived, sight unseen, at the doorstep of the apartment he shared with two other guys and announced that university housing had placed me with them. We rapidly became close buddies. After a lengthy journey through medical school, residency, and the many other hoops through which people must leap prior to being allowed to practice medicine, Steve joined a practice in Milwaukee (where he grew up). After a number of years, he left it for another one. He retired a couple of years ago.

Along the way, Steve got married and had a son.

Tragically, his wife succumbed to cancer at a very young age, and he and Sam were left alone. Within a few years, however, he met another woman, Sheryl, and remarried. They had five children together. Sheryl is a born again evangelical. She loves Steve dearly. Steve attends church with Sheryl every week and has heard countless sermons about the reality and love of God. He reads widely, too, digesting any number of books about cosmic and biological origins, always, it seems to me, looking for yet another reason to reject Christianity. He always finds one. Despite the love he finds at home and the church (the rabid political militancy of some of the congregants notwithstanding), Steve steadfastly refuses to believe in the fact of God's love.

It's difficult not to fault him. The assertion of God's love's essential presence frequently undermines how, caught as we are in our temporal frustrations, we perceive it. A number of years ago, I opened up my email to find a note from an old high school friend, a person I have known for nearly fifty years. Hippies Ruby and I once were, roaming together in the hills and canyons north of Los Angeles, Topanga, Laurel, and Malibu, both of us happily exploring and wondering what life could be. Dazzlingly beautiful, Ruby had shimmery blond hair that hung almost to her waist and a magnetic smile, a smile that invariably captivated to whomever it was directed. I thought she would be a hippie forever.

For a while, she was. Even after the Sixties were long over, Ruby continued to live the lifestyle, a woman of the hidden and wild, moving from one Indian reservation to another (she is part Native American), mountain range to mountain range, desert to desert, exploring the boundaries of her humanness. She also made and sold jewelry.

As the decades went by, however, I lost touch with Ruby. At our thirtieth high school reunion, however, we reconnected, and covenanted to keep in touch. So it was that I saw her at our fortieth reunion, too. A few months after that, I was in Los Angeles with my Aunt Jeanne, whose passing I mentioned earlier. On Saturday afternoon, while Jeanne was resting, I called Ruby. Driving up from her place about five miles to the south, Ruby picked me up and we spent an hour or so talking. Everything seemed to be good with her. After much travail and frustration, she had finally managed to sell her parents' house, which had been, for many years after they died, her home as well. She subsequently bought a much smaller house in a quirky area of West Los Angeles. It seemed a perfect fit for her.

"Billy," her email began, "I'm homeless. I had two necessary surgeries this year and because I didn't have insurance I had to sell my house to pay for them. I'm living in my car."

I was stunned. Absolutely stunned. How could this have happened?

It seemed unreal. We, all of us who knew each other in high school, had always enjoyed the fruits of our parents' affluence. We never lacked for anything. We always wore the latest fashions, took nice vacations, and appreciated our proximity to the beach. It was a golden existence.

Now all of that, for Ruby, was gone. I didn't know what to say. I wrote her back and told her that I was really, really sorry, and that I would pray for her. It seemed small comfort, really: I felt so helpless.

Because she can use the computers at her local library to send and receive email and post to her Facebook page (posts that almost always have to do with environmental and Native American issues and concerns), Ruby and I kept in touch. Occasionally, I sent her money. One day, almost half a year into her homelessness, after I read an email in which she described her constant hunger and dental pain, I took the plunge. I went theological. "Ruby," I wrote, "God loves you. God loves you very much."

Then I waited.

"God may love me," she wrote back two days later, "but I don't see it. And I sure don't feel it. Where is he?"

I couldn't argue with her sentiments: I had too often been in exactly the same place. If God and his love are indeed everywhere, we might expect to see evidence of it everywhere, too. But the seeming hopelessness of Ruby's situation seemed to indicate otherwise. Yes, as I noted earlier, God may summon a "severe mercy," but why do so to a person who is so far from him? At least a believer can fall back on her previous experience and, despite her misgivings, attempt to trust. At least she knows, on paper anyway, that there is another side to the picture.

To an unbeliever, one who had shared with me previously that, given Christianity's ugly history with Native Americans, she viewed Christianity as a genocidal religion, however, believing that God loves her is a non-starter. What reason would Ruby have to accept the love of a God whose followers had often systematically tried to obliterate any trace of her ancestors?

Never had God's presence been so present, yet never had it been so blurry and confusing.

In the early 1990s, Carol got deathly ill. I don't think she had ever felt so sick. She could barely walk. Everything ached, everything was stuffy, everything was gray. She was overwhelmed. "I know God loves me," she often said, "but this is very hard." Although after a week of medication and rest, she recovered, albeit slowly, she and I were still left to balance, and not for the first time, the conviction of divine favor with the reality of cosmic brokenness.

God's love may well be pure and true. But we take hold of it in the soiled waters of worldly contusion. It's a dichotomy that stretches faith to its limit.

But not God's. Unfortunately, however, this is often the problem.

"You had an experience of Jesus," Andre said to me as we talked in the lobby of a hotel in France, to which he and Carol, when she was working, had come for a company conference. "I'm happy for you. But it's not for me." Evidence is one thing; believing and accepting it is an entirely different proposition. I can tell Ruby that God loves her, I can tell Andre that God loves him; I can tell Fred, my college friend, that God loves him; and I can tell Brent, the youthful wanderer on his way to the Burning Man Festival, the same thing. I can tell Sherrill, Cinderella, Spruce, Lynn, Mary, David, and many more, likewise.

But what, they will say, does this mean to me? How do I know such love is real and true? As Lynn's husband Roy, who heard, probably on a daily basis, about Jesus' love growing up, shared with me, being told about Jesus' love forty years after the fact means nothing now. What's past isn't enough.

Decades ago, many years before I came to believe in

Jesus, I visited Henry, a high school friend who was, like me, in town for the Christmas holidays. I had many fond memories of Henry. Perhaps the most memorable was the night when I and two of my best friends persuaded Henry, then one of the top football players in the school, as one night we sat on a set of rarely used railroad tracks near our parents' houses, to smoke marijuana. What a wild, wild time we had. We laughed and laughed and laughed. And more. Henry would never be the same. He went on to "convert" a good part of the football team (the "jocks") to the wonders of ganja.

Now, however, Henry had found Jesus. "What are you going to do when you die, Billy?" he asked me as we talked in the living room of his grandmother's home, he the newly anointed Christian, I still the longhaired hippie. "I'll be fine," I replied, "I'll be cool."

"There's a hell, Billy. There's a hell waiting for those who do not believe."

When I smirked and smiled back at him, Henry said, "God loves you, Billy. He really loves you."

As they would do with countless more people who told me the same thing in the ensuing years, these words washed right over me. I didn't care that God loved me, I didn't care that he had died for me, I didn't care that he had a home waiting for me when I died. And I certainly didn't care that I was doomed to hell. It's a fantasy! Telling me about God's affections for me meant nothing. Even with the evidence of Henry's conversion staring me in the face.

For it had been early the preceding summer when, wanting to travel out from the beach into central Los Angeles, I decided to hitchhike. Unfortunately, I made the mistake of standing not on the curb but on the street itself, thumb out and ready. Pulling over almost the instant I did so, and quickly getting out of their vehicle, pistols at the ready and bully clubs in hand, two police officers proceeded to harass and intimidate me before giving me a ticket. "Welcome to Los Angeles," Mom said when I finally got home.

It's hard, I told Henry as in leaving I shared this incident, and too many others, with him, to see the love of God. As I noted earlier, it is oddly the very ubiquity of God's love that makes accepting its factuality so difficult. If it is indeed everywhere, then, logically, things should change. For everyone.

But they don't. The summer of 2009, when Payson and I were trekking through the backcountry of Banff National Park, deep into the heart of the Canadian Rockies, we one afternoon seemed to reach the end of the trail. We could see no way forward. What to do? First, pray. Second, check the maps which, unfortunately, were rather old (out of nostalgia, I had brought the maps I used in my original travels through this area some thirty-five years before). Happily, thanks in large part to Payson's keen sense of direction, we eventually found our way to what turned out to be the trail and, later, our campsite for that night. We liked to believe that God's loving presence helped us. But how could we really know?

Only by faith. And that, as we several days later talked with a hiker who was running out of food, is the hardest thing. Aside from seeing the visible presence of God, it is our faith, the daily working out, in relationship with God, of our conviction in his presence, that is love's evidence. Irrational? Perhaps. But if the world made absolute sense, we would not need faith. We would see. All too often, however, the world crumbles before us. Faith's crucible, and central burden, is therefore mediating between the compulsion of needing sense and the refusal to let worldly affliction make it so.

Faith's frame is far bigger than we imagine. And that is often the problem. If, as I noted earlier, God's love "surpasses knowledge" (Ephesians 3:19), we are then forced to say that it is in *not* knowing that we find our richest experience of knowing. To an age in which information is increasingly viewed as the only way to power or meaning, this seems anathema. Why should we jettison the act of knowing to experience God? Faith seems therefore to be asking us to reject who we are. It appears to dismiss one of Aristotle's most fundamental observations about the human race, an observation he made in the first sentence of his *Metaphysics,* that, "All men [people] wish to know."

This, however, misses faith's point. I believe in God's love precisely because it *does* surpass knowledge. Because it does exceed boundary, because it does outwit sensibility. Because it does, as I write in the introduction to my *Imagining Eternity,* "laugh" at knowing. I am finite. I am limited. I fool myself if I suppose I know everything about this world, if I think I can derive knowledge about this life from this life alone. I'd be running in circles. Laughing at knowing doesn't reject epistemology; it rather establishes it. Knowledge in a box only tells us what is in the box. It tells us nothing about what is outside of it.

As German philosopher Immanuel Kant put it, I "had to remove knowledge in order to make room for belief."

Nonetheless, it's a fiercely dark love, God's love is: it devours, it swallows, it wears down. It dangles me on the brink, heralding promise while undermining presence, announcing victory yet withholding its coming. But it's good. God's love is good precisely because of its darkness: it pushes me beyond what I know. It forces me to let go of what will not last, the present moments to which I so desperately cling. It calls me to embrace present epistemological murkiness even as it reminds me that through it, and only through it, I will one day see.

God's love is liminal. It is always tugging at existence's skein, always eroding its fragile carapace, ever pushing it to admit its limitations. It ends life even as it creates it, and it ends death even as it welcomes it. God's love underscores *alethia,* the truth that always is, even as it acknowledges *lethe,* the forgetting of what will never be again. Apart from life and life's end, God's love cannot fully be. God's love is a story, a story still waiting to be unfolded completely. That's its wonder, that's its complexity.

When asked whether Aslan, the great lion of Narnia, was safe, the Beaver, who was risking his life to protect Peter, Susan, Edmund, and Lucy, the four English children who had stumbled into the land, from the White Witch, responded that he was not. Not at all. But, he added, he's good.

In a broken world, God's love is one of the most dangerous pursuits imaginable. Just ask Jim Elliot. Or ask the people whom, as I have noted, the letter to the Hebrews tells us died without ever seeing the fulfillment of what God had promised them. Or someone we knew in Dallas, a member of our Sunday school class who, waiting for his fiancé at the rehearsal dinner the night before the wedding, was informed that she had just died in an automobile accident. They had waited twelve months to become one flesh. Or a friend of ours who, hearing that a missionary he and his wife had recently befriended needed a car, gave him his. He had just bought it, brand new. Or Richard Wurmbrand, author of *Tortured for Christ,* who endured the most horrific tortures imaginable to share the gospel behind the Iron Curtain. And so on.

It's a tension, a horribly bittersweet and marvelously bewildering, tension. I'm in love with a God who isn't safe, yet a God who I believe loves me infinitely. A God who "slays" me, yet a God from whom I cannot let go. If as Erasmus notes, wisdom is foolishness, I am perhaps the biggest fool of all. In every situation, I'm willing to choose to do what appears to be, from almost every earthly standpoint, the most unreasonable or, to put it in the vernacular, the totally dumbest, thing to do. It defies all common sense.

As the psalmist wrote, "Your lovingkindness [God] is better than life." (Psalm 63:3)

In an almost incredulous way, Ruby therefore had to allow herself to be even more "unsafe" to be safe. She had to believe that God is good even when her every thought and observation insisted he is not. She had to believe that the dangerous goodness she could not see, much less control, could overcome and redeem the shambles which, because she *could* see it, she deemed potentially manageable. Ruby had to tell herself that she would only find true security in God. And she had to believe it before she could see it.

It's a hard thing, this faith is. It's recalcitrant, thoughtless, and ruthless. It talks of love, but doesn't always provide its evidence. It speaks of presence, but does not always present its immediacy. It stretches us beyond limit, and invites us to treasure the darkness.

Because we believe we can see.

This is the bottom line. As I think about Ruby; as I listen to another of what Cinderella calls her "tirades" against God's absent goodness; as I remember one of my students telling me how one of his soccer teammates cursed God over his mother's death; or as I recall Sherrill's accusation that God is arbitrary and unfair, however, I find myself spinning my wheels. I cannot offer any of these people a definitive present resolution. I will always stumble against the fact of an apophatic God.

I step into answers only to find more questions.

The cruel irony, if I am to put it this way, is that issues of faith can, in some highly grating ways, become issues of infinite regress. That is, they resolve themselves by pushing us ever more deeply into the abyss out of which they come, an abyss that, by its very nature is, in this life, bottomless, without real or meaningful end. There is no present closure, there is no material solution. Nothing is brought back, nothing is returned. It's a terrible and foreboding space, this space that separates my finitude by that which defines it. It sunders, it rends. It makes me helpless, helpless before the powerful determinativity of what, in this life, will always be physically inaccessible. And absent. I will believe without ever settling the questions implicit in my belief's vision.

On the other hand, if faith were of this life only, it would be an unredeemable journey altogether.

For many years, when the high school seniors I once taught neared graduation, I had them write a "spiritual autobiography." I asked them to look back on their faith experience, or lack thereof, and think about how it had shaped them and their life. How had it changed them, what it now meant to them. Where did they see themselves, in faith or not, today, and where did they see themselves in the years to come? One year, a student wrote about an incident in her life that, outside of her family, she had shared with no one else. Emma wrote of how a few years before, overwhelmed with erotic passion for a young man she met, she slept with him. Raised to believe that sex was most properly expressed in the context of a loving marital relationship, when she stepped back from her passions and considered what she had really done, she was shook to the core of her being. Emma grew to regret her decision deeply. She began to wonder whether she would ever do the right thing again.

Eventually, Emma told her parents what she had done. To their credit, her parents did not condemn her. They didn't kick her out, they didn't withdraw her privileges. They talked to her, they prayed with her. One year later, the young man long gone, although Emma could not forget what she had done, she was slowly coming to terms with it. She believed that God had forgiven her, she believed that she could go on.

What helped her the most, however, was an observation her father made to her after Emma had shared her latest sense of travail. "Don't you think," he said, "that God is big enough for this problem?" God's no fool. He knew that when he created the world and populated it with choice making beings, he could not do so without opening the door to error and ambiguity. Equivocality is intrinsic in choice, part and parcel of finitude. As long as transcendence is present, its counterpart, immanence, will suffer from what it is.

It's a darkness of light.

When sister Kathleen wrote to tell me, shortly before she, Mom, Carol, Megan, and I were to meet for a few days of camping in Tuolumne Meadows in Yosemite National Park in the summer of 1989, that she was a lesbian, I guess I was not too surprised. Kathleen had never expressed a romantic interest in any man. She had never seemed bent on cultivating men as lovers. Although she had many good friends who were men, she had never, as far as I knew, been involved with them sexually. But I had rarely stopped to think about it either way. Many women I knew did the same. They were in no hurry to commit themselves.

One afternoon, Kathleen and I sat alongside the Tuolumne River and talked. It soon became apparent that Kathleen, like many other gay people I had known, didn't ask to have same sex feelings. She didn't wake up one day and decide to be gay. It was more of a journey, really, a journey that began many years ago, its origins steeped in an impenetrable tangle of environment, culture, and genetics. It seemed that in stating her lesbianism, Kathleen was simply giving voice to who she had been all along. She had never changed from straight to gay, nor had she always been gay. She was just being Kathleen. I'd never be able to separate Kathleen the woman from Kathleen the lesbian, nor would I ever be able to distinguish Kathleen my sister from Kathleen the human being. Kathleen will always be everything she is. As will I.

However, as I did in a letter I wrote her after I received

hers, I told her that afternoon on the river that I still could not fit her lesbianism into my worldview.

It was heartbreaking.

About four years after that summer, I decided to write an article about my experience dealing with Kathleen's lesbianism. I described how she had made me aware of it, I shared some parts of our conversation on the river, and I talked about my continuing unrest about the situation. I recounted our childhood together, how much I had loved Kathleen growing up, how much I had loved her sparkle and grace. How much I cared for her. How I loved her as my little sister.

At the end of the article, however, I was forced into ambivalence. Yes, at this juncture in my Christian journey I had problems with who Kathleen had become. But yes, I would always love her. Without really intending to, I therefore echoed one of the most tiresome, at least to me, tropes in Western Christianity: "love the sinner, not the sin."

After accepting my article, the editors of *Daughters of Sarah* invited Kathleen to write a response. They would publish both pieces together. Kathleen's response criticized, rightly so, my ambivalence. She observed that despite the extent to which I had questioned whether, in light of her disclosure to me, my theological convictions were still appropriate and true, in the end I came right back to where I started. Nothing had really changed. She added that my words to her in Tuolumne had wounded her deeply.

It was hard to disagree.

Much has changed in the over thirty years since our articles were published. I no longer worry about who Kathleen is: she is who she is. And I no longer fret unduly about her destiny. Today, Kathleen and I are the best of friends. I am so thankful. A couple of summers ago, we backpacked together, just the two of us. Does God love Kathleen as she is? He does. Would he love her more if she were not gay? He would not. God's love transcends all human boundary, disposition, and choice. Unfortunately, although this makes such love unspeakably wonderful, it also renders it enormously puzzling. I'm still left trying to measure the immutability of divine love against the unchanging fact of human freedom.

Am I slipping? Am I backsliding? I don't think so. I am simply venturing more deeply into the heavily ambiguous character of Christianity and Christian scripture in a fractious world. As I observed in my look at Psalm 139 and my thoughts on Marsha Stevens and her "Come to the Waters," if God's goodness extends into the lives of every human being, it seems as if it must extend into the lives of those who are born with the sort of structures or dispositions that might birth romantic feelings for members of their gender. Faith demands that I therefore admit that, over and against all dictum, mandate, and proclamation, I will never understand the precise exchange between human form and divine purpose.

And that I walk in a peculiar epistemological muddiness. I may have the mind of Christ, but I am also a flawed human being.

Sure, I wrestle with some of the eternal eventualities which we will all one day face, but I am more convinced than ever of the ability of God's love to make sense of them. I can't see this resolution now; I can only trust that it will, one day, come. That it will come, as will everything else about God, in the expression of his continuing presence.

But this doesn't necessarily make things any easier. Christianity is not a formula, nor is it formulaic. It is an encounter with God. And God speaks to all of us differently. This is not to condone universalism; it is just to say that, regardless of what we may think, only God knows the individual human heart. That is the wonder, that is the glory. It's also the frustration.

As faith, even as it upholds certainty, will always be certainty's counter: Ecclesiastes 3:11 all over again.

As I have noted previously, I do not understand why people are born the way they are, why some people turn out the way they do, or why some people, per Proverbs 16:4, are brought into the world for eternal destruction. In fact, I find such things enormously paralyzing. They lead me to wonder why I believe in God, to wonder why I put my trust in such a seemingly sordid paradox. Why do I adhere to such a frighteningly unresolvable framework?

Maybe because the alternative is even worse. I think that all of us, believer or not, realize that we do not live in a perfectly functioning world. We all understand that life is not always easy or fair and that things do not always go as we wish them to. We recognize that the rhythms of this universe often manifest themselves in severely damaging ways. Moreover, we all acknowledge that, as I said earlier, we "play the hand" we're dealt. We take what we've been given and move forward. Even if we do not always realize it, all of us live out Sartre's exhortation to live responsibly. We try to use our freedom carefully and wisely in what often appears to be a baffling and chaotic world. We all wish to live.

Then we die.

For many years, Carol and I have given money to Prison Fellowship, an evangelistic ministry that operates all over the world. Founded by Chuck Colson, he of Watergate fame (or infamy) after he was released from federal prison in the early Seventies, Prison Fellowship sends people, usually unpaid volunteers, into prisons to talk to inmates about Jesus. For the prisoners who come to believe in Jesus' love and forgiveness, the result is often life changing: the difference is like night and day. These prisoners become living pictures of Paul's words that, "If anyone is in Christ, that person is a new creation; the old has passed away, and all things have become new" (2 Corinthians 5:17).

From that day forward, the length or severity of the prisoners' sentence ceases to matter. Jesus is all.

Over twenty-five years ago, I was reading one of Prison Fellowship's monthly newsletters when I came upon an interview with James. In his mid-thirties, James was scheduled to be executed in the state of Texas's lethal injection facility a few weeks hence. One thing he said has always stayed with me. Talking about his belief in heaven, James remarked, "I've always wanted a home. Now I'm going to get one." As I think about James's words today, I feel immensely sad that in his brief earthly sojourn James never felt as if he had a home. I weep that he never felt wanted, never felt secure, that he always felt as if life had abandoned him. I weep that he was born into a life practically guaranteed to rupture any normalcy about existence. James never intended to kill anyone. But one night, through a set of circumstances which I will not take time to explain, he did. And now he was going to die for it.

But he knew where he was going. James believed in the active presence of God.

Was this enough? It was for James. It was enough for him to know and believe that although his earthly life had been hard, his heavenly life would be so much greater.

As to whether this is enough for you, I have no idea. Nonetheless, grace, love, and forgiveness mean very little in the absence of God. Expunge God from the universe, tear him out of every human heart, and we are left with a condemned person who, while he may feel at peace in the face of his impending execution, will, once the poison takes effect, never experience anything else again. He'll be gone, absolutely gone. Like the rest of us. God or not, the fleetingness of life is frightening, deeply frightening. And we can do nothing about it.

From every earthly vantage point, faith, faith in God's love, grace, and hope all fall prey to the raucous friction of sentient existence. However powerful and true these experiences of God may be, in the end they, too, are helpless before the certainty of death.

As I said before, it's a wild hope. We will not know absolutely until we definitively see. And then it will be too late.

One of Us chronicles the life of Anders Breivik, the Norwegian one-time video gamer and self-styled right wing pundit who in 2011 talked his way onto an island then hosting a summer youth camp and systematically killed 69 people. It was the biggest mass killing in Norwegian history. According to *One of Us,* Anders's mother became pregnant out of wedlock and, initially, considered aborting the pregnancy. But she did not.

And a future mass killer was brought into the world.

In his *Why I am Not a Christian,* Bertrand Russell stated,

> "The world, we are told, was created by a God who is both good and omnipotent. Before He created the world He foresaw all the pain and misery that it would contain; He is therefore responsible for all of it. It is useless to argue that the pain in the world is due to sin. In the first place, this is not true; it is not sin that causes rivers to overflow their banks or volcanoes to erupt. But even if it were true, it would make no difference. If I were going to be-get a child knowing that the child was going to be a homicidal maniac, I should be responsible for his crimes. If God knew in advance the sins of which man would be guilty, He was clearly responsible for all the consequences of those sins when He decided to create man."

If God knew that Breivik would turn out the way he did, why did he not lead his mother to abort him? Similarly, if he knew that Idi Amin would slaughter thousands of Ugandans, that Genghis Khan would destroy entire cities and everyone in them, or that Mao Zedong would allow twenty million Chinese to starve to death, or, well, I could go on for many pages, why did he allow them to be born? What is really going on with God's love?

It's our human freedom. We are free to accept God's love, and we are free to reject it. We are free to help others,

221

we are free not to. We are free to steward the planet with care, we are free to destroy it. It's our world, it's our life. And we wouldn't want it any other way. While one could argue that in creating the world exactly as he did, that in instituting the cosmic order precisely as he did, God ensured that murder and destruction were inevitable, this misses that he nonetheless allowed human existence to take its course. God didn't stop us from exercising our human freedom.

More than anyone, God recognizes the incalculable truth, and tragedy, of human existence: we are born, we live, we die. Though God may not like our choices, he is also acutely aware that he gave us the capacity to exercise them. He could do nothing else if he was to create us in his image. We are free beings, totally free beings.

It's deeply ironic. We shudder before, as some Jews often put it, *Ein Sof* (the infinite) or, to recall Rudolph Otto's words, the "*mysterium tremendum*," yet we quake when we realize that, apart from faith, neither might not, for us, even exist.

It's difficult to evade, completely, the point of nineteenth century naturalist Louis Agassiz's observation that, beneath it all, is the "Unnamable, the One."

Granted, as I have noted numerous times in this meditation, I will never reconcile the fact and consequences of human choice with the fact and consequences of God's absolute sovereignty. I'll never understand, in this life anyway, how these come together. To the end of my days on this planet I'll struggle to align God's constancy of love with life's continuing capriciousness and my limited ability to understand and respond to both.

Hence, as I review the many legacies of human history,

I see all too many instances of my fellow humans engaging in behaviors that leave me aghast. Behaviors that cause me to weep bitterly, that cause me to despair of humanity completely, that make me wonder why we're even here. Behaviors that make me tremble at the purpose of the human race.

Behaviors that occasionally cause me to wonder if there really is a God.

On the other hand, I crater similarly before the staggering complexity of a love that, although I trust it implicitly, I nonetheless do so in the grip of a compelling freedom to ignore it altogether. As I have affirmed more times than I can count. God's love may well be seminal, pervasive, and present, yet it is also mine to win or lose, choose or cast away. It will not inhabit me unless I ask. It will not happen unless amidst the darkness, the awful and perplexing darkness of who I, a human being created in the image of God, am, I trust God.

The irony or, some might say, cruelty, is exquisite. Occasionally I wonder if, all things considered, we really would be better off if people like the Assyrian king Sennacherib, the Mogul warlord Timur, the Indian ruler Asoka before he converted to Buddhism, the Marquis de Sade, Josef Stalin, Pol Pot or, to name everyone's perennially favorite example of human sin, Adolf Hitler, had never lived. Would we be the same people we are today? Would we have as much insight into the human heart? The human mind?

I can't possibly know. On the other hand, I believe that God rejoices at the lengthy compendium of human achievement, the inventiveness and brilliance, the remarkable powers of creativity and imagination that have brought the human species to what it is today. Even if, I might add, such brilliances manifest themselves in people who have totally rejected God. After all, he made *all* of us.

So I trust. I trust that somehow, some way, God's purpose will prevail. And that it is good. But it's a two way street: trust is truth as much as it is sorrow. I've loved Led Zeppelin's music for decades. When I was barely seventeen, some friends and I drove from our beachside suburban homes to the legendary Rose Palace (where, you guessed it, the Rose Parade, that long revered display of New Year's saturnalia, begins) in downtown Los Angeles to see Led Zeppelin perform. The band did not disappoint, rocking the stage for what seemed like hours, Jimmy Page dazzling us with his guitar work, Robert Plant wailing as only Robert Plant could do, John Paul Jones stoically thumping on his bass, and John Bonham, drummist extraordinaire, pounding out every beat, his long hair tossing madly in the smoky (not from cigarettes) room. It was a vision of rock 'n' roll bliss. We did not get home early that night. In fact, it was in the wee hours of the morning when we finally stumbled into our respective homes, our parents long asleep or, in the case of my poor mother, lying awake until her wayward son returned safely.

A couple of years later, when Zeppelin released its iconic "Stairway to Heaven," a song that would dominate the top of the music charts for literally decades to come, I listened and danced to it endlessly. I never tired of hearing it, never wearied of catching the opening notes of Page's double necked guitar. So this song played as one day in the spring of 1972 I talked with a group of friends of my eagerness to get to the Brooks Range in northern Alaska. Together we wondered about what I would do when I saw one of the many grizzly bears that populate that remote arctic wilderness. I should be careful, they told me; perhaps, some said, I shouldn't even go. "Stairway" mused to us of words without meaning, winos by the road, the lady who buys a stairway to the stars, its every word serving to accentuate the enticing terror of the enormously desolate character of the range I planned to explore come summer. For I would indeed be totally alone, completely cut off from all help and assistance. It would be worlds different from the trek I had taken just a year earlier, when I embarked on a two week trek across some of the highest peaks of the Sierra Nevada. After the first day, I saw no one else. On the second day, I encountered a storm that lasted days. No one came for me, no one talked to me. No one knew where I was. As I tromped on and on, day and night, through continuing deluges of rain and too close strikes of lightning, I was well aware that no one, absolutely no one, knew that I was doing so. Not even the animals: they had all fled for the lower elevations. I felt as if I was the last person on the planet.

Now I'd be *on* another planet. And whether God was there, or not, wouldn't matter one bit.

Many years after Zeppelin had done its last concert, its unity fractured irreparably by the premature death of drummer John Bonham, I read a book called *Hammer of the Gods*. In perversely compelling detail, *Hammer* describes the inside story of the rise and fall of Zeppelin, the intensity with which they did their music; the countless women they enjoyed; the lurid tales of the wanton destruction they unleased on many a hotel room around the world; and more. One chapter, a chapter that described the writing of

"Stairway," however, left me wondering. At the time that Plant and Page wrote the song, Page was living in the house on Loch Ness (home of the legendary sea monster) which, some decades before, had been owned by British mystic Aleister Crowley.

Around the same time that I read *Hammer,* I read a biography of Crowley. I read of his journey into the dark arts, his deliberate entanglement in the chthonic battles of the supernatural. I also read of his travels, his many travels to find the deepest and darkest enlightenment. He even attempted to climb K-2. As I did with *Hammer,* I found it perversely fascinating.

"Whatever is met," Crowley often said, "do what thou wilt." Whatever you wish to do, it is right. So do it. Do it regardless of consequence, present, future, or future to come. Do it knowing that you're stepping into the horror of an eternal hell, do it knowing that as the traitorous Judas of the musical "Jesus Christ, Superstar" puts it, you'll be damned forever. And more: it doesn't matter.

Crowley's tombstone perhaps puts it best. As he requested, it read, "And now the silly bastard [Crowley] is on the shelf, we'll bury him beneath another sod."

There was really no point to begin with.

Yet God's love says that Crowley's life matters as much as yours and mine. That it matters as much as that of Who drummer Keith Moon who, according to a friend of a friend, worshipped Satan; that it matters as much as that of Pol Pot, Stalin, or Timur. Today, the three remaining members of Zeppelin continue to live and do music. And God continues to love them, past indiscretions and all. Robert Plant, Jimmy

Page, and John Paul Jones will live until as Robert Plant put it in a recent interview, "The curtain comes down."

What always and always weighs on me, however, is that as much as I enjoy Zeppelin's music, one day I will, in a way I cannot now know fully, be beyond it. But the three living members of Zeppelin, well, they may not.

It's sometimes so very difficult, and painful, to grasp the nature of infinite love in a finite world.

Writing, over a hundred years ago, in his monumental *Great Chain of Being*, Arthur Lovejoy observed that according to the medieval principle of plentitude, the world cannot be endlessly diverse without there being a corresponding endlessness of evil. That is, plentitude demands plentitude in every way, every aspect, every dimension of existence. Put another way, the logic of the world demands that, oddly enough, we cannot do without evil. Evil is essential to realizing a complete world.

It's quite befuddling. And it's made even more befuddling in that my only way out of it is to trust the one who created this world.

And to know that he will never give me any definitive answers.

One day, my dear friends, people like Sherrill, Cinderella, Spruce, and Linda; people like Mary, Hank, David, Margaret, and Jeff and Harlan; and many others, will die. One day, they will bid farewell to this life, this momentary slip of physical existence. They will be gone from this planet forever. As will I.

God, however, will be as present as he has ever been. His love will remain. As will eternity. I find this profoundly uncomfortable. I love that my friends have been free. I love what they have done with their lives. I love that we've been a part of each other's time on this planet. I love these things almost more than life itself. I cannot imagine my life today without having known them.

Yet God may well find their spiritual choices unacceptable. And unlike the highly fluid eternal fates of Hunahpu and Xbalanque, the trickster twins of Maya legend, human destinies are ordered by God. There is no appeal. Why therefore is it that when humans exercise one of the most precious components of their creation in the image of God they are in fact potentially removing themselves from permanent union with the one in whose image they are made?

Why must earthly freedom lead to eternal despair?

And why if, as Keith, one of my atheist friends, once asked why although we are free to decide that we do not want a God interfering with our lives, this God will, in the end, interfere anyway? In the many years since I graduated from high school, I've tried to attend every ten year reunion my class has celebrated. Although I missed my tenth (held the summer I worked on Cape Cod), I traveled to my twentieth, my thirtieth, fortieth, forty-fifth and, soon, I will travel to my fiftieth. The committee of my high school classmates that plans these reunions is much invested in these events, and meets regularly to discuss them. I'm grateful. And thanks to Facebook, all of us stay in close touch.

But even with Facebook, I don't catch everything. One member of the committee has made it her job to track those of our classmates who, sadly, die. Every reunion the list grows longer. And the poster on which she displays the graduation photos of the deceased has become two.

Soon, I fear, Paula will need to set up three poster boards to accommodate the number of photographs of the fallen.

I make it a point to visit these boards. I want to see, I want to remember. I want to remember who these people were, what they were like, what they meant to me in my high school days. I want to rejoice in their part in my life.

I also want to let myself be torn by the senselessness of death and dying, to deepen my melancholia about the human adventure. I want to confront my human limits. At my fortieth, the photos of two classmates in particular, two classmates by the name of Doug and Steve, shouted at me. What wild times we had together, with what brashness we once strode across the fields of our Sixties adolescence. So many hours of cultural anarchy and revolutionary debauchery. We did it all, Doug, Steve, and I; we did everything that we could possibly do. Because we could.

We were free.

And, I realized as I pondered Doug and Steve's youthful visages on the poster board, as much free to live as to die. When I saw Doug at our twentieth, he displayed the effects of his freedom. I could barely make sense of what he was saying. He was a no show at the thirtieth, but I didn't see his photo on the poster board. Though I didn't see Steve at our twentieth, I heard about him at the thirtieth, that he was doing well. Now they're both gone.

As to where Doug and Steve are today, I have no idea. Only God knows their heart.

Vexingly, however, as only God had granted them this freedom, so only God was present at its end. All of us lived, Doug, Steve, and I, and now I'm the only one who remains. While my freedom continues, theirs is over. Whatever else happened, for Doug and Steve, matters have eventually settled into the eternality of God. And what can any of us do? Freedom is who we are, but freedom is, ironically, the road to what we are not, too.

Like the characters in a Pieter Bruegel painting, we live lives suspended between human longing and divine will.

In an almost exasperating way, however, that is God's love.

I hope that one day I will see Doug and Steve again. I hope that one day I can dance with them once more. I hope that one day all of us will understand why we have been given freedom that ends us. I hope that one day I will know why God gave me freedom to believe in him when for so many years I chose not to. I hope that one day I will see why he made me as he did.

I hope that one day I understand the fullness of God's love.

But I'm not holding my breath. A resolution of eternity is just that: eternal. Try as I might, I cannot now picture it fully. Infinitude bursts all categories of present sense and sensibility. Ironically, although apart from God's love I would not know of these eventualities, apart from God's love, I would not even be here. It's a curious measure of happiness.

I've talked about the book of Job many times in the course of these reflections. I now return to its final chapter, chapter forty-two. Here, newly humbled by God's assertion of his sovereign power and mastery over all things, Job adopts a new posture before his creator. Having been thoroughly pummeled in his body, and now likewise in soul, Job tells God that, yes, you're right: I really do not know who I am before the overwhelmingness of your power. I'm lost, he says, lost in the most bitter of places, the intimacies and longings of my heart. I realize I have no inkling, not even a semblance, of the vision undergirding and sustaining this existence.

"Hear, now," Job says, "and I will speak; I will ask You, and You instruct me" (Job 42:4). I trust you, God. I trust you fully.

But what a hard road to reach this point! When, as Luke's gospel relates, the angel Gabriel informs Mary, the future mother of Jesus, that she, betrothed but not yet married, would become pregnant *before* her wedding day, she of course wonders. The Jewish tradition in which she had been raised held, had in fact held for centuries, that unwed persons should refrain from sexual relationship. Yet here was an angel of God, a messenger from the divine One, telling her that she would soon experience what is the direct result of sexual relations. Moreover, in the little town in which she was then living, Mary knew that her pregnancy would rapidly become common knowledge. And she knew that when this happened, she could be cut off and ostracized or, worse, stoned as an adulterer.

What's on God's mind?

Living as we are in the twentieth-first century, entrenched in an ethos committed to arriving at logical understandings of every event, person, and thing, had we been recipient of such an experience, most of us would likely want to pepper Gabriel with questions. We would want to know more. We would wish for more information about why.

Or we might dismiss him completely.

According to Luke's account, however, Mary only

asked one question. "How," she said, "will this be?" As a person who had been raised to believe implicitly in God's lovingkindness and faithfulness, Mary had no reason to doubt Gabriel's word. Sure, she may well have wondered— who would not?—but she set her questions aside and simply asked Gabriel how this "thing" will happen. In other words, Gabriel, I believe you. Just tell me how this will come to be (see the full account in Luke 1:26-38).

Before Luke tells Mary's story, he writes about Zacharias. Zacharias, the husband of Elizabeth, was a priest who had all of his adult life served faithfully in the temple in Jerusalem. Both he and Elizabeth, Luke says, "were righteous in the sight of God, walking blamelessly in all the commandments and requirements of the Lord." Yet they had no offspring: Elizabeth apparently did not have the ability to bear children.

One day, as Zacharias was performing his priestly duties, Gabriel visited him. You will have a son, Gabriel told him, a son who will prepare his people for the coming of Messiah (Jesus). Although he was surely as confused as was Mary when she heard that she was to become pregnant, Zacharias had a different response.

"How will I know this for certain?" he asked, "for I am an old man and my wife is advanced in years."

Unwise words. Angry over what he deemed Zacharias's lack of faith, duly infuriated that he would not accept this divinely empowered news without wondering whether it would actually happen, Gabriel struck the hapless priest mute. You will not speak again, he told him, until your son (whom, he had already told him, was to be named John), was born (read the account in Luke 1:5-20).

If we draw a line from Job to Mary to Zacharias, we see a number of intriguing contrasts. In delivering his final soliloquy, despite his endless complaining throughout his ordeal, Job never asked God why. He simply acknowledged that God is who he is.

So it was for Mary. She hadn't suffered the physical indignities and spiritual setbacks of Job, nor had she engaged in Job's bold pushbacks against the value or rightness of God's activity. Nonetheless she, like Job at the end of his frightful sojourn, realized that, faced with the reality of God's presence, mediated as it was through Gabriel, she had nothing to say. She did not, should not, need to ask why. God is. That was all she needed to know.

Zacharias, however, saw things differently. God's presence, again, as it was mediated through Gabriel, wasn't enough for him. Zacharias needed to know absolutely. He needed some concrete assurance that what Gabriel was predicting would actually happen.

Hebrews 11:1 notes that, "Faith is "the assurance of things hoped for, the conviction of things unseen." Faith is being convinced in the absence of evidence. It's specifically *not* being certain. Faith is security in the midst of insecurity. Faith does not hang on deeds, it does not cling to outcomes. It does not fall prey to emotion. Faith is a decision. It is a conscious decision to trust the presence of God.

And, and this is a BIG "and," it is a decision to trust that in this presence, this seminal fact of God's presence, a persevering and eternal love is always working. Always.

It's the biggest decision of all.

And it's in the dark.

I've talked about predestination, I've talked about cancer.

I've talked about vocational anguish, I've talked about job endings. I've talked about being lost, I've talked about being found. I've talked about exclusivity, I've talked about sin. I've mentioned conundrum, I've mentioned vexation. I've pointed to purpose, I've pointed to meaning. I've told of joy, I've shared of hope. I've talked about mountains, volcanoes, deserts, and oceans. And triathlons. About Islam, Buddhism, and Judaism; about music, waterfalls, and creation. I've spoken of moment, I've spoken of eternity, and life and death and everything that fills them. And I've talked about the music that always plays. I could probably go on for tens, perhaps hundreds of pages more. The experience of faith, as I have known it, is endless. It's endless not only because it is an earthly experience grounded in a heavenly eternity. It's also endless because it asserts certainty in an uncertain world. In the midst of a highly unpredictable existence, faith continues to insist that truth and certitude remain. In this life, faith will therefore always struggle. Vexation and ambiguity are givens.

Do we then do as Bertrand Russell, who counseled his readers to build their lives on what he believed to be the "scaffolding of despair?" Or as biologist William Provine, who realized that, without a God, we are nothing more than evolutionary plops? Or as physicist Steven Weinberg, who observed that the more he understood about the universe, the more he realized how pointless it is? And so on.

At the memorial service we held for Mom a few weeks after her passing, all of us, Bob, Ellen, Kathleen, and I, spoke. I was last. I drew on the final verse of Psalm 90 which reads, "Let the favor of the Lord be upon us; and give permanence to the work of our hands; yes, give permanence to the work of our hands" (Psalm 90:17). Like all of us, I said, Mom sought to live her life in a way that would ensure its permanence, that would ensure that her life had mattered for a good that would outlive her. And that she had succeeded. In many ways. But unless we set this verse into the first one of the psalm, I added, her efforts, and all of ours, are in vain. "Lord, You have been our dwelling place in all generations. Before the mountains were born or You gave birth to the earth and the world, even from everlasting to everlasting, You are God" (Psalm 90:1-2).

As I write, I'm listening to Joseph Haydn's "Creation." I shared earlier one of its most famous parts, "The Heavens Are Telling the Glory of God." Are they? "Look out the window," a student said to me many years ago, "and you know that God exists."

If you believe. Or as another student once shared with me, "I just *know* that God exists!"

Does she? Poet Samuel Taylor Coleridge once suggested, "Read the first chapter of Genesis without prejudice, and you will be convinced at once [of the presence of God]."

Maybe so. As I have noted, however, belief comes with considerable baggage. It raises questions of epistemology, it raises questions of ontology. It raises question of logic. In the end, however, it's still a matter of trust. Do I or do I not trust God, a God whom I can't see or hear or prove definitively to be whom he claims to be?

But a God who changed—and continues to change—my life, and the life of billions of others, in so many wonderful ways. That's the bottom line.

"I know that's what you believe," my neighbor Russell said to me one night as we ate dinner together. We had been conversing about the historical validity of the Bible. I argued for it; Russell the opposite. But historical evidences aren't the real point of faith, are they?

Not really. While evidences are critical and essential points for faith, they are not *the* point. The real point is that faith, in all its glory and perplexity, is the door to a relationship with God. Faith is to trust an invitation of God for relationship, an enduring relationship of faithfulness and love.

When I was about ten years old, I went with my grandfather (whose passing I mentioned earlier) on a guided tour through a cave in the western edge of Sequoia National Park. At one juncture in the tour, the ranger led us into a large cavern, and encouraged us, all thirty or so of us, to stand still. Then he turned off the lights.

Never had I "seen" such blackness. Though I could sense my grandfather's presence, mostly because I assumed he was still there, I could not in any way see him. I feared that had I turned around (he was standing behind me), he would vanish. It was very frightening.

Although the ranger only left us in this darkness for about twenty seconds, it seemed like a lifetime. I was beginning to think I would never see anything again.

As I move on through the rest of my life, I look back often, not out of nostalgia, but out of wish to glean lessons learned. Of lessons learned about trusting God, of lessons about living, day in and day out, with the frequently disturbing darkness of light. Of lessons about the hiddenness of hope and grace, about the inscrutability of a loving and invisible God. And more. I see, see over and over again, that faith isn't necessarily a way to see. Or understand. Faith is a way to live, regardless of what life is. It's a way to live with God.

Very early on, I shared some thoughts of Bertrand Russell about God and good. As I stated, I cannot "prove" that God is good by saying that, well, he is good. And I'll never be able to fully unravel the complicated question of God's oversight and human choice. Once again, faith isn't about proof. It's about trust. Yes, as I have said, I can cite evidences, empirical evidences for the presence of the supernatural in human experience, and yes, I can offer ample testimony to the power of this presence to shape and direct the behavior of rational people. I absolutely use my reason in my faith. But I cannot now, and never will at any time in the years to come, be able to accept any of these things without trusting, in less than clear light, that they are true. Aquinas was absolutely right: reason alone will not reach or define God. I will always need to make a conscious decision to trust what I cannot fully understand. And I will need to do this until the final moment of my final day.

In the closing scenes of Steven Spielberg's *Indiana Jones and the Last Crusade,* Indiana, played by Harrison Ford, is on the verge of finding the legendary "Holy Grail." A number of obstacles, however, stand before him. I will focus on the last one. Indiana finds himself standing at the end of a tunnel on one side of a bottomless abyss. The way to the inner sanctum, and the Grail, lies on the other side. But there's no bridge. Indiana therefore must, as his father, played by Sean Connery, has told him repeatedly, "believe." He must believe that when he steps out over this abyss, a path will appear. He must have faith.

Steeling his heart and closing his eyes, Indiana steps into the void. And a path appears.

"Lovingkindness and truth (faithfulness) have met together," Psalm 85:10-11 intones, "righteousness and peace have kissed each other. Truth springs from the earth, and righteousness looks down from heaven." Above and beyond all my nagging doubts, endless questions, and persistent bewilderment, my faith is to trust the void, the void of darkness that is light. To trust it for the meeting, the meeting of my heart and mind and soul with the love of God.

And live.